THE GAMBLER
a screenplay

THE GAMBLER

a screenplay by

Katharine Ogden & Charles Cohen
and
Nick Dear

Methuen Film

Published by Methuen

Screenplay copyright © 1997 Trendraise Company Ltd.
Introductions copyright © 1997 Nick Dear, Marc Vlessing, Jodhi May,
Karoly Makk, Charles Cohen
Stills photography: Ferenc Markovics, György Kaláski

The authors have asserted their rights under the Copyright, Designs and Patents Act,
1988 to be identified as the author of this work.

First published in the United Kingdom in 1997 by Methuen,
Random House, 20 Vauxhall Bridge Road, London SW1V 2SA

Random House Australia (Pty) Limited
20 Alfred Street, Milsons Point, Sydney,
New South Wales 2061, Australia

Random House New Zealand Limited
18 Poland Road, Glenfield
Auckland 10, New Zealand

Random House South Africa (Pty) Limited
Endulini, 5A Jubilee Road, Parktown 2193, South Africa

Random House UK Limited Reg. No. 954009

A CIP catalogue record for this book
is available from the British Library

ISBN 0 413 72890 0

Typeset in 10 on 13.5 point Plantin Light
by Deltatype Limited, Birkenhead, Merseyside
Printed and bound in Great Britain by
Cox & Wyman Ltd, Reading, Berkshire

CONTENTS

INTRODUCTION

CHARLES COHEN
(WRITER)

In the spring of 1989, I was in New York. A friend invited me
to the screening of a movie at the Public Theater. The film
was *Another Way* by the eminent Hungarian director Karoly
Makk. By the end of the week, I had seen five of Makk's films
and numbered myself among the converted.

My friend knew Makk and made the introductions. We met
a second time at a house in the Catskills. All hell was about to
break loose in Eastern Europe and Makk was eager to discuss
the coming storm. Hearing his perspective on Gorby and
Boris only confirmed how little we Americans understand the
Russian mind.

Still, I mentioned a project that had been in the back of my
mind for some time. It's a story that takes place in Russia,
about a brilliant writer on the verge of securing his place as
the world's foremost novelist. One small problem: a compul-
sive gambling habit that leads him to a Faustian pact with an
unscrupulous publisher. His only hope a young, female
stenographer, serious but conventional, to whom he dictates a
new novel. The young woman falls in love with the middle-
aged writer. In the process, she discovers that art and life can
indeed converge. In the end she becomes the gambler, risking
all for love. That the story is true and the writer Fyodor
Dostoyevsky would only help to raise the stakes.

Makk knew the story and offered his encouragement. Later he would provide notes. Thus I began to write the screenplay with my collaborator, Katharine Ogden. The first step was paring biographical material as rich in drama as any fiction. The facts are well-known: Dostoyevsky's trial for treason against the Tsar, his mock execution, his years as a political prisoner in Siberia, his return to St Petersburg to resume his career as a writer. There, hounded by the censors, chronically short of money, he fled Russia for the spa towns of the continent, not to take the cure but to indulge his passion for roulette. He was a regular at the casinos of Baden-Baden, Wiesbaden, and Marienbad – names synonymous with the overripe luxuries of a dying class and era. At his side was the beautiful Polina Suslova, twenty years his junior, an obsession as compelling and as doomed as his gambling.

When Suslova finally threw him over for a young, handsome Spaniard, Dostoyevsky returned ignominiously to St Petersburg. He was forty-four years old, epileptic, debt-ridden, and a widower. His beloved brother Theodore was dead; Theodore's family had to be cared for, adding to Dostoyevsky's financial burdens. Not surprisingly, Dostoyevsky resumed his gambling. Only now his IOUs were bought up by an unscrupulous publisher called Stellovsky.

In desperation, Dostoyevsky signed a contract with Stellovsky. The novelist was paid 3,000 roubles for a new novel to be delivered within the year. Failure meant Stellovsky would gain the rights to all of Dostoyevsky's work for the next nine years. The value of the penalty clause went up considerably when Dostoyevsky's latest work *Crime and Punishment* hit the kiosks in serial form. The novel was an instant hit. Everybody loves a good murder story. The public clamored for more, but *Crime and Punishment* had to be put aside. Dostoyevsky owed Stellovsky a novel and the deadline was a month away.

Dostoyevsky confessed his dire situation to a friend who recommended a young graduate from the new stenography school in St Petersburg. Her name was Anna Snitkina. She was hired on the spot and Dostoyevsky dictated *The Gambler* to her in three weeks, depositing the manuscript at a lawyer's office with two hours to spare. Dostoyevsky liked the new method of composition so much that he employed Anna to help finish *Crime and Punishment*. Within a few months they were married.

Dostoyevsky's new-found success and happiness did not keep him from gambling. Destitute once again, he and Anna fled to the continent where Dostoyevsky continued to play roulette. Anna pawned her jewels to pay his debts, nursed him through his epileptic fits, tended to their two children, both born in German spa towns, and took dictation. With her help, Dostoyevsky was able to complete two more masterpieces, *The Idiot* and *The Devils*.

Finally, the couple returned home to St Petersburg. Dostoyevsky quit gambling. Anna managed his business affairs while continuing to take dictation. Her calm efficiency and loyalty prompted Tolstoy to comment: 'If we had all married Anna Snitkina, we would have all been Dostoyevsky.'

Dostoyevsky's *The Gambler* is both richly autobiographical and consistent with the themes of his greatest novels. In its exploration of the borders of human personality, the novel exposes Dostoyevsky's central belief that the mysteries of human nature are revealed in its excesses and obsessions – a conviction reinforced by the conditions under which the novel was conceived and composed.

My intention was never to do a traditional film adaptation of *The Gambler*. There had already been Russian, French and English versions of the novel. What interested me was the story behind the novel, the relationship between Anna and Dostoyevsky. Here was a conventional young woman, inexperienced in life and love, suddenly thrown into the strange, seductive world of the tortured artist. As Dostoyevsky dictates the novel to her, Anna discovers that the novel's tragic hero

(Alexei) and heroine (Polina) are alter-egos for Dostoyevsky and his former lover Polina Suslova. By now it is too late to stanch her burgeoning feelings for Dostoyevsky. Can she save him from his demons? And at what cost to herself?

The screenplay presented certain challenges. We were attempting to tell two stories at once with the novel a counterpoint to the life, interweaving them in such a way that they would inform each other. Striking the proper balance was essential, which meant presenting enough of the novel for the audience to care about its characters and understand its themes. We wanted them alternately shaken by the tragedy of Alexei's spiralling obsession, then stirred by the Anna/Dostoyevsky love story culminating in Anna's actions to save Dostoyevsky from his demons.

To this end we created a fictional confrontation between Anna and Polina Suslova. At the critical moment – as the novel spirals toward its tragic conclusion and the relationship between Anna and Dostoyevsky finally heats up – Polina Suslova suddenly appears to reclaim Dostoyevsky. Anna's worst fears are confirmed: the tragic hero of the novel is Dostoyevsky's alter-ego; Alexei's dual obsessions of sex and gambling mirror the author's own obsessions; Suslova's seductive power suddenly threatens Anna's position.

Throw in a ticking clock as Stellovsky's deadline approaches and we knew we had the possibility for a thrilling ending. Can Anna save Dostoyevsky from the same tragic fate that befalls the young hero of the novel? Can they deliver the manuscript in time to thwart the cunning Stellovsky? In the end will Anna choose a frenzied existence with a tortured genius over the safe, conventional life of a bureaucrat's wife?

These were risks enough for all to take. The thrill was in spinning the wheel.

NICK DEAR
(WRITER)

No writer could resist this story. You've signed a lousy
contract, you have to deliver a new novel or lose all rights in
your work, and with a month to go to the deadline, you
haven't begun. Even better when the procrastinator in
question is one of the great names of Russian literature –
Fyodor Dostoyevsky. Even better when the story's true.

After I had recovered from my initial burst of euphoria – it
being always a comfort to know that other writers, even great
names of Russian literature, also screw up their schedules – I
put to the producers and director these questions: did they
wish to focus on Dostoyevsky's novella *The Gambler* itself, or
on the conditions in which it was written? Would it not be
more productive to take one theme, or the other, instead of
attempting this rather tricky commingling of the two? The
answer came back unequivocally: No, it wouldn't. The thrust
of the story was to be precisely the interrelation between the
writer and his writing – an exploration of the process itself,
with all its fortuity, mystery, and mundanity.

It's become a commonplace of literary criticism to down-
play this curious symbiosis between the author and the work,
and to stress the 'stand-alone' nature of a text without
reference to the circumstances of its creation. Up to a point,
this is fine. You can certainly read Arthur Miller's *The*

Crucible and decide for yourself whether it's a good play or a bad play. Once you know, though, that it was written at the height of the anti-communist witch-hunt in the USA, and that the author himself suffered not a little discomfort in the face of this, you see the drama in a different light. Between the world of work and the college tutorial, the gap yawns wide.

Anybody who picks up a computer in the morning to ply their trade knows that what you write that day will be influenced by factors such as toothache, bank statements, world news, successful love affairs, unsuccessful love affairs, or that letter you've been expecting from the Nobel Prize people. The words don't come by themselves, unless you have some of that sophisticated American screenwriting software. And when time's running short and you've got to deliver something – anything! – you may find you fall back on that story you don't need to research. The one you know. The one you've lived.

My guess is that Dostoyevsky, faced with an almost impossible task, did just that. He took as his source material his own great guilty secret: gambling. Yet the book he wrote is – let's face it – thin. It bears the marks of a thing written in haste, especially towards the ending, if there was one, which there isn't. It springs to life, however, given a little background. Once we know that the man was hazarding his entire living on this turn of the wheel, the inconsistencies of the book become increasingly irrelevant, whilst its themes surge to the surface. The addiction to roulette, for its own sake, for the pain of losing as much as the pleasure of winning; the fascinating, hurtful, temperamental lover; the debauched young Russian male, symbol of the country's spiritual degeneracy ... it's an impressionistic canvas, imprisoned in a realistic framework. To succeed, it *needs* to be seen in context.

This thinking forms the basis of our film.

MARC VLESSING
(PRODUCER)

How would you describe *The Gambler*? It is in many ways an unusual film to have been made today. It is not another English costume drama about repressed sexuality or the eternal class struggle. Its atmosphere is European, but it is not what the Americans would call a foreign-language film. Karoly Makk is not a new 'hot' director waiting to be discovered by the international critics. The producer's task is made harder still when you add to these considerations the fact that the script has a complex structure with two narrative lines. All of this explains why it took over five years to get this film off the ground. But these features all had their positive side: the originality of the script and the presence of a director with a clear vision and a wealth of experience became the reasons why it was made.

My involvement began in June 1992 when an acquaintance handed me a copy of Katharine Ogden and Charles Cohen's early draft of the script. The story's premise has been described elsewhere in this volume so I will not repeat it here, but I was struck by the opportunity it offered to explore how Dostoyevsky's obsessive and destructive world could collide with the altogether purer and more innocent world of Anna. The story's double structure was the extra challenge.

Remarkable though I felt the story was, I also knew that it

would be very hard to finance. The first difficulty to overcome with prospective financiers was to convince them that we knew how to balance the two stories and that there was actually a point in so doing.

We were often asked why we could not just make a film about Dostoyevsky and Anna's love-story, but we felt that writers make for boring biopics. Others tried to drive us into the direction of a straightforward adaptation of the novella, yet the whole point of this script was to create a multi-faceted storyline in which life and art would drive each other forward and create a satisfying whole. Unsurprisingly, it took us close on three years to develop the script.

Early on in the process, in 1992, I received a letter from Channel Four questioning whether it was appropriate for them to become involved in 'a Russian period piece'. The writer went on to say that '. . . even as a gambler myself I found it hard to draw much contemporary relevance from the story as presented here . . .' It is a matter of some irony that Channel Four later became this film's most enthusiastic champion and indeed its vital promoter. But, essentially, that letter summed up all the difficulties which lay ahead. It also helped us to prepare our answers. Why, after all, should English-language period films be restricted to eighteenth- or nineteenth-century Britain and who could question the modern resonances of a compelling love-story, let alone one set against the background of obsessive gambling?

I was told by other producers never to develop a story in a vacuum, but as the curt rejections kept piling up we had no choice but to keep working on it without proper feedback. It was the European Script Fund's life line of some development money which made us feel that we had something others could care for; their early support was crucial.

Later, on the strength of Karoly's film *Love*, David Aukin at Channel Four came on board and committed to developing the script with us. Karoly was the ideal director for *The*

Gambler, it was essential to have someone with an Eastern European, as opposed to a pragmatic Anglo-Saxon, point of view. There were a number of additional attractions in working with him. First, he is probably one of the world's best directors for depicting women intelligently and sensitively, a rare skill amongst film directors. Second, he knows how to hold the camera still when it matters. *The Gambler* is a very fast-moving script which could have tempted a less experienced director to rush through it. We felt the film was all about creating stillness. Karoly also has the ability to amplify seemingly simple moments and look at them from the most complex angles; equally, big problems are capable of being reduced in his hands.

Together with David, we engaged Nick Dear to work on the script and it was his fresh approach and feeling for the material which shaped it into something that became properly focused.

One of the more complicated aspects of developing a script with four lead roles (Dostoyevsky, Anna, Alexei and Polina) and two narrative structures is whether the director, producer, writer and financier believe that they really are talking about the same project. In fact, much of the shared vision which we developed came out of the casting process. For a long time we wanted to cast the same actor for Dostoyevsky and Alexei. Alexei is clearly Dostoyevsky's younger *alter ego* in the film and by having the same actor playing both roles, we felt that the audience would more readily assume the interweaving of the two stories. The problem with that approach was that we could only agree on a couple of actors who had the range to play the two characters with equal confidence. More problematically, those who we felt could handle both roles were all in the big-budget bracket and turned us down anyway.

Interestingly, many people who have seen the film in pre-release screenings before its general release have commented on how closely Michael Gambon and Dominic West resemble each other. I can honestly say that by the time we cast them, we had completely given up on the idea of creating any physical likeness between their characters. The fact that Dostoyevsky and Alexei coalesce in the mind of the audience is because the script subtly draws upon the similarity between the characters and because the actors and Karoly were mindful to create that bridge.

Our casting director, Celestia Fox, was a loyal and staunch supporter of the project throughout. One day she was due to have lunch with Anthony Hopkins and in advance asked us whether we would be interested in showing him the material. There was not much discussion really. Hopkins would, we felt sure, make a wonderful Dostoyevsky. To my astonishment, he wanted to do it. Two weeks later, Karoly and I were sitting in his living-room in Chelsea, with Charles waiting on the phone in America to hear the result. When I called him to say that Hopkins was keen, albeit that he had a very short timetable for the project, there was euphoria mixed with the realisation that making the film was now within our grasp – and that was daunting!

During the winter of '95, whilst walking over Hampstead Heath, Charles and I agreed that with Anthony Hopkins attached we could afford to set even more ambitious production values and lengthen the overall shoot. But with the same speed with which Anthony Hopkins joined the project, he removed himself from it. Oliver Stone persuaded him to do *Nixon* and his new agents decided that that was just the right thing for him to turn his career to. Gone was Hopkins and gone too was our hope of getting *The Gambler* made. With Anthony Hopkins attached, financing the film had been relatively easy. With him gone, the offers of finance miraculously disappeared.

Having been administered a dose of realism about the machinations of large talent agencies and their star actors, we went back to the drawing-board. The rescue came indirectly.

As we had to find a new way of funding the picture, setting it up as a European co-production involving at least three countries was the only way of finding enough money and tapping into sufficient subsidies to get the project funded. I had always wanted to work with the Dutchman, Ben Van Os, as the set designer for this film, having been very impressed by his work on *Orlando*. I also had the good luck of executive producing a film with a Dutch director of photography, Jules van den Steenhoven, whose lighting I thought was exceptional.

Karoly was confident that some Hungarian finance could be found and, as a Dutchman myself, I set about trying to find a Dutch co-producer. Robert Swaab and René Seegers liked the project and could see a way of raising quite a substantial amount of money from the Dutch market. Throughout the making of the film they were an important influence on the whole project.

We revisited the schedule and the locations and cut back in order to find a balance of production values which we could fund within the confines of a European co-production. The decision to shoot the film in Hungary was guided by the fact that we were fortunate to find a castle complex in western Hungary which could double as Roulettenburg. Also, working with Karoly simply opened doors in Hungary which for most other foreign producers would have been firmly shut.

Re-casting Dostoyevsky was very difficult. True, there was the image we now all held of Hopkins in that role, but equally there simply are not that many male actors in their late forties/ early fifties who have the ability to play such a complex character and combined with sufficient drawing power to bring in an audience. When Michael Gambon accepted we celebrated!

All the other main casting decisions followed on quite naturally. We were all convinced that Jodhi May had the gift to portray the depth, fragility and ultimate strength which all combine in the remarkable character of Anna Snitkina. Polly Walker had always shown an interest in Polina and was keen to join us when we finally got the film off the ground. Dominic West was so obviously made to play Alexei that we could not imagine anybody else in the role.

Finding Grandmother, however, was a challenge. Karoly mentioned Capucine, which got us all quite excited until we discovered that she had died five years previously. Various agents suggested a range of British actresses, but none of them convinced us as forceful Russian matriarchs. We met Luise Rainer through her agent. Karoly and I made an unforgettable visit to her London flat to persuade her to break her fifty-year retirement. She was formidable and absolutely right for the part. She also had the interesting effect of dramatically reducing the age gap between Karoly and myself, as we sat in front of her like two shy schoolboys! One of the challenges for me as a producer throughout the shoot, and in preparing the film's release, has been to accept that Luise used to work with the likes of Louis B. Mayer; we all had a tough act to follow.

The Gambler was a project full of risks: would the double structure work, would Karoly take to directing a large cast in English, how would it be to work with Luise after such a long absence from the big screen? The joke on the set when faced with a difficult decision was that we had taken endless risks before and so we might as well continue taking them. The decision about the editor and overall editing style of the film was a continuation of the same policy. Kevin Whelan had a strong reputation in commercials, but the difference between cutting a commercial and cutting a feature film is similar to that of the sprinter versus the long distance runner. Whilst we all agreed that the narrative structure of the film would be helped by reasonably aggressive editing techniques, the first edit contained too many jump-cuts and dissolves. Karoly's early training was as an editor and his passion for shaping the material, combined with Kevin's brilliance, made for a powerful team. Together, they created the film's own visual language and one which, in my opinion, has served the story well.

I will miss *The Gambler* as a project. A first film is an astonishing experience and I know that I will never feel as strongly the urge to make a film again. This was a script which I pitched hundreds and hundreds of times to Americans, Japanese, French, Germans – you name it, they got the pitch. To some, I pitched it as an adaptation of Dostoyevsky's novella – an exploration of an important piece of European culture and its background. To others, it was shamelessly pitched as a sensual love-story, erotic and passionate. A producer ultimately has to do whatever it takes to make those who are inclined to invest sign their cheques. We all worked on *The Gambler* with great ambition and I can say that everybody involved did their utmost to create a special and remarkable, European film.

JODHI MAY
(ACTOR)

When I first read the script of *The Gambler* I was immediately attracted to the way in which it explored the relationship between the biographical detail of the writer's life and his work. As an actor, what made the role of Anna particularly attractive was the progression she makes from the naïve girlish figure we see at the beginning of the film, to the more assertive woman who is capable (in the script at least) of becoming part of the writing process itself at the end of the film. In this respect I was struck by the unusual nature of the relationship between Anna and Fedya, and the way in which the script sought to juxtapose, the unconventional nature of their love with the conventional romantic heroism of Dostoyevsky's literary heroes, Alexei and Polina, by interrelating fact and fiction. What I saw in Anna was a sense of intrigue and curiosity; a desire to experience the very things which Dostoyevsky writes about, a desire to live through fiction in order to escape the limitations of a mundane quotidian life. For Anna, I believe it is this capacity to enter the fictional world of Dostoyevsky's imagination that not only enables her to understand him to the extent that she does, but draws her to and results in her falling in love with Dostoyevsky himself.

On arriving on location in Budapest I was very nervous, having come straight from Oxford where I had been studying without so much as a day's break in between. Although I had managed to fit in a small amount of reading before I arrived, most of it was done during the week of rehearsals, so on first encountering Michael and Karoly I felt somewhat unprepared. We started rehearsing the day after, and on meeting Michael I have to admit to being a little intimidated. Quite apart from his imposing appearance, I was apprehensive of the prospect of working with someone who I not only had a great deal of admiration and respect for, but who had such an enormous amount of experience. However as soon as rehearsals started a combination of Michael's constant smoking and swearing, brilliant humour and genuine warmth put me at ease, and I continued to find Michael one of the most generous and giving actors I had ever worked with. During rehearsals Karoly, Michael and I blocked the scenes chronologically (a luxury that only rehearsals allow) and went on to discuss each scene individually, pin-pointing what each one was about, in order to create a map of the relationship between Anna and Fedya from its beginning to its end. However the rehearsal period was short and kept to a minimum as I think Karoly wanted to keep everything as fresh and spontaneous as possible for the camera.

The first three weeks of shooting were done in a studio not far from where we were all staying. It was a studio which had obviously seen a lot of cinema history in its day as the hallway walls were covered with black and white photographs from famous Hungarian films of the forties, fifties, and sixties, some of which were from Karoly's own films. One in particular was from a film of Karoly's called *Love* which I had seen before arriving in Budapest. The film was about a woman who nurses her husband's dying mother while he is in prison. Without the heart to tell his mother that her son is a political prisoner, she reinvents her husband's life as a famous film director who travels to America and writes the most enchanting letters to his mother about his success. At the end of the film we discover that the letters have been written by his wife, and on the day of his release, the letters having stopped, his mother dies. The photographs on the studio walls recalled the fact that like Karoly himself, it too had survived communism by producing politically subversive films thinly disguised as Romance – only to make the successful transition from the old system of unlimited state-funding to a new commercial industry of tight budgets and love stories.

It was in this studio that Fedya's study had been recon-structed. The study itself was small, and the atmosphere one of intimacy and concentration. The surrounding decor cre-ated a cloistered environment. The set was draped with heavy, embroidered fabrics, and on its walls hung a collection of Russian icons, and paintings of enlarged, garish, human faces copied from Goya. The crew was, for the most part, Dutch and Hungarian and, despite the difference in language, was an unusual but extremely friendly team. Although speaking the most excellent English, Karoly directed with the help of an interpreter, which enabled him to use both languages whilst directing. On one occasion this caused an embarrassing incident in which I listened with attentive concentration as Karoly described in Hungarian the erotic nature of a particu-lar scene we were about to shoot, using a fairly explicit analogy relayed through his interpreter, blushing at his description. I looked up to find that a hushed and silent crew had been listening with equal concentration and attentiveness. However, on the whole language was never a problem and I enjoyed working with Karoly enormously. As a director he was particularly sensitive to the needs of his actors and encouraged me to take Anna in a direction that was more courageous and forthright than I had envisaged. On first reading the script I had imagined Anna as more reticent and withdrawn, yet what Karoly was able to draw out was a feisty, confident and driven woman, able to channel and direct Fedya's creativity.

During the course of the first week's shooting Karoly and I discussed the importance of establishing a sense of growing intimacy between Anna and Fedya as their relationship progresses. What I realised, throughout the course of shooting, was the need to emphasise the contrast between Fedya's tired pessimism and sense of futility and Anna's youthful optimism and determination. As Anna warms to Fedya, she becomes intrigued by him, and fascinated by his work. There are key scenes in the script in which we see Anna's changing attitude towards Fedya, which Karoly and I had discussed in rehearsals. The most important moment in terms of conveying this process, from my point of view, is the prayer scene where Anna kneels down and prays with Fedya. Karoly wanted the scene to be played with great pathos and reverence, and yet for it to be kept simple, in order to preserve its subtlety, so he asked us not to make eye contact. As a result what unites both Anna and Fedya in this instance is the sensibility which they share implicitly, as Anna is able to observe Fedya in a moment of intimacy and vulnerability. The same effect is created in the seduction scene, where Fedya reads to Anna over her shoulder observing her growing desire as he caresses her. In this respect it was extremely exciting to work with a director who was continually trying to find new ways of shooting a scene, and Karoly's approach helped us to feel more at ease with those that centered upon the love, and more specifically, the sexual attraction between an older man and a younger woman, to the extent that the physical intimacy of these scenes felt, and I think looked, very natural.

Whilst shooting I had been given a book by Marc in which there were two photographs of Anna; one of her as a young fresh-faced woman of about twenty, around the time that she would have met Fedya, the other of her as an older woman of probably forty. The difference between the two images of Anna was striking. As a young woman she appeared supremely confident, good-looking and somehow innocent. As an older woman she appeared still confident and good-looking yet almost bitter. However striking this impression was it was important to resist the temptation to think of Anna as borne down by the will of a strong man; instead I saw her as someone who had an equally strong will of her own. In this sense Karoly and I felt it was important to play on a more light-hearted side of her character by introducing an element of farce into the scenes between Anna and Stellovsky. This enabled us to inject a sense of comedy and coquetry into her character in order to steer away from this impression of Anna as a stern, long-suffering woman. Again it was this sense of comedy that was to govern the way Michael and I played the later study scenes where, ever closer to the deadline, Anna collaborates with Fedya in writing the last pages of the book, giving the scenes added energy and spontaneity, as Karoly allowed our joking to spill over into the takes.

When shooting in the studio was completed and we reconvened in the exterior locations, it felt very disorienting and strange to have lost the intimacy and quiet focus that the study had allowed. Without the chronology of the study scenes it became increasingly difficult to envisage the sequence of events which were shot piecemeal. This however is the standard drawback for any actor on any film of working on location, due to the fact that there is so much more moving around involved. What struck me most in this particular instance was the way in which during the scenes in the gambling hall, where Anna comes to collect Fedya, it felt as though we were shooting a completely different film, surrounded by the worn faces of Roulettenburg. Once I had seen a completed version of the film, I was astonished by the extent to which the real and the fictional elements of the script had been so cleverly interwoven, intercutting between the dark, sombre interiors of Dostoyevsky's study, and the bright, garish colours of Roulettenburg. It was then that I was able to perceive Karoly's vision of a carefully balanced interplay between fact and fiction in terms of dramatic and visual genres. In this respect Dostoyevsky's literary game of approximating fact and fiction through the confessional tone of *The Gambler*'s narrator seems to me to have been perfectly appropriated to the medium of film.

KAROLY MAKK
(DIRECTOR)

When Fyodor Dostoyevsky – accompanied by his wife Anna, who is carrying their baby in her arms – leaves the casino in Roulettenburg after losing the family's last penny and asks for forgiveness with an impotent gesture to his beloved, she can only say: this is your fate and I accept it.

But until then – the last scene in the film – young Anna and the genius writer have to take up their roles in an unbelievably rich and capricious life.

Anna – a twenty-year-old modern woman (or rather, girl), who has been placed near the middle-aged writer by her teacher, and about whom she only knows the same hearsay as any other citizen of St Petersburg – realises she has been locked in a dark, mysterious flat with this at times charmingly clever, and at other times desperate, helpless, strangely-behaving epileptic, who is in a hopeless position because of the well-known bet with his publisher – that he must write a novel in twenty-eight days or forfeit all rights to his future works. Sometimes with artfulness, sometimes with ruthless humour, he shows her those secrets of her life that, for the twenty-year-old girl, are frightening, unintelligible, sometimes revolting, but an adventure of a lifetime. It is as if Dostoyevsky only dictates this book so that Anna can encounter all those passions: gambling, love, sex and the sense of power which they bring; passions which she will struggle with for so much of her life.

There have been many comparatively faithful adaptations of Dostoyevsky's *The Gambler*. In our movie the novel is simply an occasion to create a different love story between Anna and Dostoyevsky.

Anna eagerly and curiously waits for those stories to come to life in Dostoyevsky's fantasy, as we did when we were young and we wished to ambush the big secret, the naked body of a woman through a drilled hole of a countryside log cabin. It feels as though the old writer tells Polina, Alexei and De Grieux's strange and exciting love story to trap this innocent girl. She doesn't know it yet but this trap has been set in her body and soul for a long time. Her fate is just waiting for her to take her there.

Anna and Dostoyevsky's relationship is almost the antithesis of the love story in the novel. Their love is born from small events, almost unnoticeable gestures, the slow getting to know each other's being and feelings, the pressure of interdependence, leading to the finale of passion and opening up.

I wanted to show a love story in which the world of fantasy impregnates and brings to life a love which happens in twenty-eight days in a dark and tiny flat in St Petersburg between a locked-in woman, Anna, and a man, Dostoyevsky. Please do not look for any hidden philosophical depths or heights behind this seemingly complicated film; I am interested in love, gambling and money.

My vision of the film can be seen from the above notes. All of cold St Petersburg is in the dark, prison-like flat. In the flat an infinite dimness, a strongly-lit corner here and there, a grey dawn still finds this strange couple working or half asleep. Then the peculiar stories of fantasy which fly out like colourful birds – the summer season in a German spa town, the colonnades of a Grand Hotel – and then back to this dark flat.

For Anna this is a fatal and strange story; we see through her eyes that the life of Roulettenburg is too rich, too colourful, too strange: the glittering dresses of the people, the glimmering red of the Casino, an almost otherworldly light, the power and resolution in Grandmother's eye.

Two visual worlds will struggle with each other, not to win one over the other, but to give more for the viewer.

Budapest, May 1996

THE GAMBLER

GRAND HOTEL. DAY.

A splendid hotel in a German spa town and gambling resort.

CAPTION: *'Baden-Baden. 1870.'*

PAWNBROKER'S SHOP. DAY.

ANNA, *in her mid-twenties, worn and frayed beyond her years. She removes a diamond ring carefully from her finger and hands it to the* PAWNBROKER. *He bites on it and weighs it. Then he throws it down.*

CASINO ENTRANCE. DAY.

ANNA, *with a* CHILD *on her arm, approaches the casino. It looks like the entrance to hell: garish red lights, plush doors leading into a secret nether world, thick with sweat, smoke and the smell of money.*

CASINO. DAY.

ANNA's *eyes scan the room, searching for someone amongst the legions of gamblers. With the* CHILD *on her arm she walks past dozens of* GAMBLERS, *some wretched, some ecstatic, all focused on the roulette tables which dominate the room. Chandeliers hang low over the tables. It's dark, murky, indisputably evil.*

ST PETERSBURG. DAY.

A horse-drawn cart passes along a muddy street.

CAPTION: 'St Petersburg 1866. A true story.'

STENOGRAPHY SCHOOL. DAY.

We see a different ANNA: *young, fresh faced, alive, untroubled by cares. She wears bright colours, and smiles a lot.* ANNA *stands in the doorway and looks around, searching for someone. It's the Stenography School in St Petersburg. She passes a classroom in which a group of* STUDENTS *watches a* PROFESSOR *explain the principles of shorthand with the aid of a blackboard. Most of the* STUDENTS *are young women.*

PROFESSOR: Remember, the ultimate purpose of the system is to enable you to provide a clear and concise transcription of the text. This should be written out as soon as possible after the dictation has been heard. You should never delay.

    ANNA *enters the next room and sits down at the desk opposite her friend* DUNYA, *who works at a typing machine. They speak above the clatter of the typewriters.*

DUNYA: Did you see Ivan last night?

ANNA: Yes – he walked me home.

DUNYA: And? Did anything happen?

ANNA: Nothing interesting.

DUNYA: Nothing at all?

ANNA: No. Fairly ordinary evening.

    DUNYA *looks down at her work.*

ANNA: I nearly forgot. He proposed.

DUNYA: He proposed!

    They laugh happily. A SECRETARY *comes into the hall. She calls out:*

2

SECRETARY: Anna Snitkina! Professor Ohlkin will see you in the library.

LIBRARY. DAY.
ANNA *sits opposite the good-natured* PROFESSOR OHLKIN *in the high-ceilinged library.*

OHLKIN: Now, how is your father's condition? Is there any improvement?

ANNA: No. He is worse. The doctor says any day now.

OHLKIN: This morning I had an approach from a friend, who has a friend, who is an author. This gentleman requires a stenographer immediately, for one month. The pay is fifty roubles.

ANNA: Fifty!

OHLKIN: Will you take it?

ANNA: Yes! Thank you!

ST PETERSBURG, COURTYARD. DAY.
A rather dingy courtyard. ANNA *and* IVAN, *a pleasant but dull young man, are standing under an umbrella in the rain. They examine a strange building – interesting but depressing at the same time. It's elegant but decrepit.*

IVAN: Not exactly a good address.

ANNA: Well, he's an author. They prefer places with atmosphere.

IVAN: I don't like leaving you here.

ANNA: Ivan, my family needs the money. It's only for a month.

IVAN: Have you – reached a decision?

ANNA *looks blank.*

IVAN: My proposal.

3

ANNA: I'm sorry. I've been so busy, I've barely had a chance to think.

IVAN *looks down.* ANNA *smiles.*

ANNA: Kiss me.

IVAN: When one is married one may kiss in public. I think . . . a little discretion.

IVAN *takes a cigarette from a case and is about to light up.*

ANNA: Ivan!

ANNA *takes the cigarette from his mouth and throws it to the ground.*

IVAN: If we marry there will be no need for you to work.

ANNA (*flares up*): Look, married or not, if I want to work, I shall work!

ANNA *goes towards the door.*

IVAN: Got your notebook? Pencil? Pen? Ink?

ANNA: Yes!

ANNA *enters the building. She closes the door behind her. A* SHIFTY MAN *watches from a doorway, holding a newspaper.*

DOSTOYEVSKY'S APARTMENT. DAY.

ANNA *walks up the stairwell, eyes wide with anticipation. The door is ajar and she pushes it open. She tentatively enters the apartment. It's a strange place. Dimly lit, and somehow mysterious: a new world. A handsome young man, the same age as* ANNA, *comes out of a doorway:* PASHA. *He's dressed in an Arabian silk gown, with pointed slippers, and a silk scarf around his head. He smokes a cheroot in a long, ivory holder. He peers with curiosity at* ANNA. *He's attractive, if a little weird.*

ANNA: Mr Dostoyevsky? I've come about—

PASHA *puts a finger to his lips and then points further*

along the hallway, towards an open door. ANNA *walks forward. From inside the study comes the voice of* FYODOR DOSTOYEVSKY (FEDYA), *who is arguing with three* CREDITORS.

FIRST CREDITOR (*shouting*): I implore you to settle this now.

FEDYA: I don't care how many credit notes you have! I can pay no one!

FIRST CREDITOR: You have paid no one for six months, sir!

SECOND CREDITOR: This cannot go on indefinitely!

    ANNA *watches from the adjoining room.*

FEDYA: My brother's widow depends on me! I have to feed her children!

FIRST CREDITOR: Your brother's widow is not my concern. If these notes are not met with interest—

FEDYA: What are you trying to do? Ruin me completely? Get out! Get out! Out!

    The CREDITORS *leave the room.*

FEDYA: Get out! Don't come back!

SECOND CREDITOR: Insufferable man!

    FEDYA *notices* ANNA.

FEDYA: Another one! How much do I owe you?

ANNA: Mr Dostoyevsky?

    FEDYA *is twenty-five years older than her. He puffs violently on a foul-smelling cigarette.*

FEDYA (*seeing her folio*): What is that? A summons? What, are you trying to bleed me dry?

    He turns back to the CREDITORS *who are lingering in the hallway.*

FEDYA: I have to write, write. It's only by writing you will get paid, you understand? Now get out!

SECOND CREDITOR: We'll be back!

    The CREDITORS *leave.* FEDYA *coughs. He looks at* ANNA *over his spectacles.*

FEDYA: So, my creditors are sending schoolgirls now, are they? Think they can butter me up with a pretty face? (*He bawls into the hallway.*) Ustinya! Where's my tea? (*To* ANNA *again.*) This place is a madhouse. Why are you still here?

ANNA: It's eleven o'clock. I understood I was expected.

FEDYA: I expect no one. I have to write. Please go!

ANNA: I understood I was to assist you in that. My name is Anna Snitkina. Professor Ohlkin sent me.

FEDYA: I've never heard of him. I have to write. (*Calls.*) Ustinya! Tea!

ANNA: He is a professor at the School of Stenography.

FEDYA: You are a stenographer! Ah! I apologise. Fyodor Mikhailovich Dostoyevsky at your service.
He takes her hand and attempts to kiss it. ANNA *pulls away her hand.*

ANNA: I would rather you didn't. I think those old rituals do modern women a disservice.

FEDYA: Oh really? Well, I have no interest in what you think. You are here to take dictation, nothing more. It was a courtesy, that's all. Do you think I'm trying to seduce you?
He motions her to go through to the study. As he customarily would, he stands aside to let her go first. Then he deliberately barges in front of her.

FEDYA: I'm so sorry, I forgot. Modern women!
ANNA *is working hard to suppress her fury as she follows him into the study.*

FEDYA: Please, sit down.
ANNA *sits. The study contains a large desk, a smaller table, a couch on which* FEDYA *sleeps, piles and piles of books and papers. The shutters over the large windows are permanently closed.* ANNA *takes out her notepad and pencil and looks up.*

FEDYA: So, how does it work?

ANNA: We use the Gabelsberger System.

FEDYA: German?

ANNA *nods.*

FEDYA: I hope I don't have to speak German, do I? Well, let's give it a try. But I have no confidence in this. No confidence at all. It's all too late. Too late.

He lights another cigarette.

FEDYA: Are you ready? (*Dictates.*) 'My name is—'

ANNA: Excuse me sir, what are we writing? I need to know how to set it out on the page. Is it a business letter?

FEDYA *looks at her as if she is mad.*

FEDYA: A business letter? I do not write business letters. Are you a complete imbecile?

ANNA: Professor Ohlkin says I am his best student.

FEDYA: We are not in the land of Professor Ohlkin. We are in the land of literature. Literature. (*Suddenly very gloomy.*) Oh, why am I wasting my time with all this? I have failed, that's all there is to it. I've failed.

He sits down with his head in his hands.

ANNA: Please, give me a chance?

FEDYA *sighs, stands up again and starts to dictate.*

FEDYA (*very fast*): 'My name is Fyodor Mikhailovich Dostoyevsky. I am forty-five years old. I am the author of, amongst others, *Poor Folk* and *The House of the Dead.* In the year 1850 I was exiled to Siberia as a political prisoner. I served four years in a prison camp in Omsk. I served the next four years as a private soldier in Semipalatinsk, near the Chinese border. Semipalatinsk is a town of six thousand souls; in Semipalatinsk there is one piano. In 1859 I was privileged to return to St Petersburg, by the gracious mercy of the Tsar, whom God preserve.' Read it back.

He's gone so fast that ANNA*'s pencil has been flying as*

*she struggles to keep up. She's very nervous as she begins
to read.*

ANNA: 'My name is Fyodor Mikhailovich Dostoyevsky. I
am forty-five years old. I am the author of *Poor Folk*
and *The House of the Dead.*'

FEDYA (*angrily*): 'Amongst others, comma, *Poor Folk* and
The House of the Dead.'

ANNA (*corrects her text*): You went so fast . . . ! (*Reads.*) 'In
the year 1850 I was exiled to Siberia as a political
prisoner. I served four years as a private soldier in
Semipalatinsk, near the Chinese border.'

FEDYA: What about Omsk?

ANNA: I beg your pardon?

FEDYA (*fuming*): Omsk – what about Omsk? I served four
years in a prison camp in Omsk. And you omit it
from my life! Gabelsberger system – pah!
*FEDYA storms out. In the hallway he walks past
USTINYA who's bringing the tea.*

FEDYA: You drink it!
*ANNA sits in silence, miserable. PASHA, dressed to go out,
appears in the doorway.*

PASHA: Well, that was very clever. You have offended
Papa and you've driven him out in a rage. And now I
have no money for the day. Do not imagine you are
welcome here.
*He leaves, closing the door. ANNA stares bitterly after
him. Then she throws down her pencil.*

CAFE. DAY.
FEDYA *is at a table with his friend* MAIKOV, *a well-dressed,
affable poet. They are drinking champagne.*

FEDYA: Twenty-seven days.
MAIKOV: It's not easy.

8

FEDYA: Twenty-seven days! And one of them wasted
     attempting some ridiculous system of shorthand.

MAIKOV: Shorthand? It's catching on in Europe, I hear.

FEDYA: It might be catching on in Europe. It's not
     catching on with me.

MAIKOV: Fedya, you can't do this on your own. I've
     spoken to a dozen writers, all good: Plinskov,
     Zerinsky, Golyadkin—

FEDYA: Any Nihilists?

MAIKOV: No.

FEDYA: Thank God for that.

     FEDYA *drinks more champagne.*

MAIKOV: Here's my plan. You give us your outline – your
     structure, your character notes – and we will write a
     chapter each. You do the first and the last. The
     deadline is the crucial thing. What do you say?

FEDYA: It is a generous offer but I cannot do it.

MAIKOV: Why not? The consequences will be—

FEDYA: To hell with the consequences, Maikov. I cannot
     put my name to something I haven't written.

     FEDYA *holds his head in his hands. He moans.*

MAIKOV: Are you ill?

FEDYA: It's the champagne.

COURTYARD. DAY.
The SHIFTY MAN glances at his pocket watch as FEDYA
staggers through the courtyard.

DOSTOYEVSKY'S APARTMENT. DAY.
FEDYA *hands his overcoat to* USTINYA *and goes into the*
study. He lies down, tired, on the couch. ANNA *is sitting*
patiently at the desk. She gets up and offers him a sheet of
paper.

9

ANNA: I have prepared a clean copy of your dictation, sir. Perhaps you would care to check it?

FEDYA *takes the paper, puts on his spectacles and reads it through. He's impressed.*

ANNA: Are there any mistakes?

FEDYA: No. (*He examines her carefully.*) You need this job?

ANNA *nods.*

FEDYA: Are you ready?

ANNA *smiles. She immediately sits and picks up her pencil.*

FEDYA (*quickly*): 'I am returning to Roulettenburg, after an absence of two weeks. It hasn't changed.'

GRAND HOTEL, ROULETTENBURG. DAY.
It's the hotel we glimpsed at the beginning. A carriage approaches it, through the magnificent garden.

FEDYA (*voice-over*): 'The little town on the Rhine is still famous for its mineral waters, its casino and, of course, the Grand Hotel.'

A young Russian, ALEXEI, *sits in the carriage.*

FEDYA (*voice-over*): 'This is where our party is in residence.'

The carriage pulls up to the entrance of the Grand Hotel. ALEXEI *jumps out. He watches as his party returns from a carriage ride. First, the* GENERAL *helps* BLANCHE *down from the carriage and walks her towards the hotel. She's showing a fair degree of décolletage. They hold drinks in their hands.*

FEDYA (*voice-over*): 'The General, my employer, is a man who is determined to play roulette until he has squandered his entire fortune. He loses money every day. Yet he keeps finding more from somewhere.'

ALEXEI *takes up his suitcase and moves towards the side*

entrance, watching them discreetly.

FEDYA (*voice-over*): 'Mademoiselle Blanche, his friend, is a
– well, let's just say she's French.'

From the other carriage, BLANCHE*'s mother,* MADAME
DE COMINGES, *descends, helped by* DE GRIEUX, *who
then turns to* POLINA *to help her out as well. Two*
CHILDREN *walk away with* MADAME DE COMINGES.
GROOMS *hold their horses as they dismount; the* HOTEL
STAFF *serve drinks.*

FEDYA (*voice-over*): 'And Madame de Cominges, her
mother, is a comtesse – she says. Well, perhaps she is.
And perhaps her friend, de Grieux, really is a
marquis. Perhaps.'

DE GRIEUX *turns back to let* POLINA *take his arm.*
They follow the others, lazily sipping their drinks. DE
GRIEUX *is a dandy, strong and powerful, with all the*
confidence that money brings. ALEXEI *watches them from*
behind a pillar.

FEDYA (*voice-over*): 'And there's Polina. She sent me to
Paris on private business. But something's happened
whilst I've been gone. Look at the way she smiles at
the Frenchman. She smiles, because she knows I'm
watching. But I think she is in trouble. I will have to
save her.'

POLINA *looks up and sees* ALEXEI. *She holds his gaze.*

DOSTOYEVSKY'S STUDY. DAY.
ANNA*'s hand, writing fast.*

ANNA: 'Save her . . .'
FEDYA (*voice-over*): Full stop.

FEDYA *sits on the couch, smoking.*

FEDYA: Do you think the hero will save her?
ANNA: Well, that is what the hero normally does, isn't it?

GRAND HOTEL, ALEXEI'S ROOM. DAY.

ALEXEI *is unbuttoning his shirt.* KARL, *a bellboy, pours water into the wash-basin.* ALEXEI *is looking out of the window.*

KARL: You are with the General's party?

ALEXEI: I tutor his children.

KARL: An educated man.

ALEXEI: Educated and broke.

KARL: Try the casino.

> ALEXEI *bends down to the wash-basin and looks through the window.*

ALEXEI: What's it like in there?

> KARL *follows his look.*

KARL: It's fantastic. It is the only true democracy in Europe. Everyone is equal before the spinning wheel.

GRAND HOTEL, CORRIDOR. DAY.

DE GRIEUX *and the* GENERAL, *in riding clothes, walk along the hotel corridor.*

DE GRIEUX: I give you two more weeks, then I foreclose on the mortgage.

GENERAL: Three years ago I broke the bank. I can do so again, I know it.

DE GRIEUX: You have no further collateral, mon cher. How can I lend you any more?

GENERAL: Please, monsieur, my mother is very, very ill.

> *They stop outside* BLANCHE*'s bedroom. She is leaning against the door-frame and watching them.*

DE GRIEUX: Is she?

GENERAL: Let her be my collateral.

> BLANCHE *comes out of the doorway.*

BLANCHE: Ah, mon Général.

GENERAL: Ah, Mademoiselle Blanche.

12

She strokes the GENERAL*'s collar.*

BLANCHE: I cannot take off this beautiful pair of boots by myself. Would you be so kind as to help me?

The GENERAL *clicks his heels and walks into her bedroom.* BLANCHE *exchanges a discreet glance with* DE GRIEUX.

DOSTOYEVSKY'S STUDY. DAY.

FEDYA *leans on his desk with a cigarette in his mouth.*

FEDYA: What kind of a novel do you think this is?

ANNA: I can't decide if it is a love story, or a story about roulette.

FEDYA: Which would you prefer?

ANNA: Well, I was brought up to believe that gambling is immoral.

FEDYA: And love, you think, is all moonlight and roses?

ANNA *looks down for a while and shakes her head.*

ANNA: I don't know what it is.

FEDYA: It is suffering. Pain and suffering. Next chapter.

ROULETTENBURG. DAY.

ALEXEI *walks through a field full of flowers.*

SUMMER-HOUSE. DAY.

POLINA *is sitting in the summer-house. She looks up as* ALEXEI *enters.*

ALEXEI: Did you miss me?

POLINA: Don't be silly. (*Impatiently.*) Did you pawn my jewels?

13

ALEXEI *holds out a fine ladies' handkerchief which is knotted into a small sack.* POLINA *grabs for it, and they giggle. She unties the handkerchief. Inside are a few gold coins which she eagerly counts. She's disappointed.*

POLINA: It is only seven hundred!

ALEXEI *shrugs.*

ALEXEI: Paris is flooded with diamonds.

ALEXEI *holds up a pair of ornate earrings. This angers* POLINA.

POLINA: I told you to sell those.

ALEXEI: Do you remember what Grandmother said when she gave these to you? She said you were the only one who could wear them, the only one proud enough . . .

POLINA: Seven hundred francs – it's not enough.

ALEXEI: Why do you need so much money?

POLINA: I just need it. That's all. Without it, I am a slave.

ALEXEI: To whom? De Grieux?

ROULETTENBURG, PARK. DAY.

ALEXEI *looks at the* GENERAL*'s party promenading through the park. He follows them from a distance. Everywhere people are gaily dressed, the sun shines, a brass band plays a military march. The* GENERAL *is with* MADAME DE COMINGES. DE GRIEUX *walks next to* BLANCHE, *behind them.*

DE GRIEUX: Now is the time.

BLANCHE *walks quickly ahead towards the* GENERAL.
MADAME DE COMINGES *steps aside.*

BLANCHE: Mon Général. (*She takes his arm.*) It is so sad. Your mother is definitely unwell?

GENERAL: Oh, definitely, definitely. Three days ago we heard that she was declining, and yesterday that she had died! The news came from Sergei Petrovich, in St

Petersburg, and he's a reliable man. But I cannot confirm it.

MADAME DE COMINGES: Why not send a telegram, General?

GENERAL: What, and ask if my mother is dead?

DE GRIEUX *contrives to walk next to* POLINA.

DE GRIEUX: Are you related to Grandmother, Mademoiselle Polina?

POLINA: The General is my stepfather. There is no blood connection.

DE GRIEUX: But nevertheless, I expect you will be mentioned in Grandmother's will. She likes you, no? And her fortune is vast, so everyone says. Oh, you will inherit, I feel sure.

He smiles at her. From a distance, ALEXEI *watches them.*

DOSTOYEVSKY'S STUDY. EVENING.
ANNA *puts her things in her bag and stands up.*

ANNA: What time would you like me tomorrow?

FEDYA *laughs in surprise.*

FEDYA: Tomorrow? No, you cannot go. We have only just begun.

ANNA: Well, I can start early if you wish.

FEDYA: No, no, you cannot leave. I do not work office hours, do you understand?

ANNA: I may not go home?

FEDYA: There is a room here. I'll send Ustinya tomorrow for your clothes. I need a stenographer for one month. If you want the work, you stay in the apartment.

DOSTOYEVSKY'S APARTMENT, LANDING. NIGHT.
ANNA, *clutching her folio, follows* USTINYA *upstairs.*

DOSTOYEVSKY'S APARTMENT, ANNA'S ROOM. NIGHT.
USTINYA *shows* ANNA *into a tiny maid's room upstairs.
There is a little bed, with an icon on the wall above it, a
chest, a washstand; nothing else.* USTINYA *leaves.* ANNA *sits
disconsolately on the bed and looks around her, with a heavy
heart.*

DOSTOYEVSKY'S STUDY. NIGHT.
FEDYA *lights a cigarette, pacing the floor.*

ANNA'S ROOM. NIGHT.
ANNA *sits up in bed, dressed in her shift, staring at the wall.*

DOSTOYEVSKY'S APARTMENT. NIGHT.
ANNA *leaves her room silently and goes downstairs.*

DOSTOYEVSKY'S STUDY. NIGHT.
FEDYA *sits behind his desk, struggling inwardly with his work.*

DOSTOYEVSKY'S APARTMENT. NIGHT.
ANNA *walks through the dark apartment. She enters the
dining-room. The remains of* FEDYA'*s supper are still on the
table.* ANNA *begins to eat the leftovers. She is starving.
Bending over to get some more food, she knocks over a chair.*

DOSTOYEVSKY'S STUDY. NIGHT.
FEDYA *looks up.*

DOSTOYEVSKY'S DINING-ROOM. NIGHT.
ANNA *holds her breath. Nothing happens. She continues eating.* FEDYA *enters silently.*

FEDYA: I have begun the next chapter. Come.
He turns back to the study. ANNA *follows with the plate of food.*

GRAND HOTEL, BELL TOWER. DAY.
Roulettenburg. The setting sun bathes the garden and fountains in a golden light. ALEXEI *stands close to* POLINA *on the balcony of the bell tower.*

ALEXEI: Please tell me what's going on. Are you in love with the Frenchman?
POLINA: Alexei, you must do something for me.
ALEXEI: Anything! My life is yours. I place no value on it.
POLINA: Don't be ridiculous.
ALEXEI: I was never more serious! Tell me right now to throw myself off this tower and I'll do it.
ALEXEI climbs on to the balustrade.
ALEXEI: Go on, say it! 'Jump!'
POLINA: No! I need you.
She takes his hand and pulls him down.
POLINA: Take this and play roulette. Win as much money as you can for me.
She pulls out the bunched handkerchief from her dress and thrusts it into ALEXEI*'s hands.*
ALEXEI: Why?
POLINA: Just do as I ask, if you love me.
ALEXEI: But I don't want to gamble!

POLINA: You must. You said you'd throw yourself to your
death! I need money. I need to be free.

ALEXEI: I would like to set you free!

POLINA: Then win for me at the tables.

She kisses him passionately and leaves. He sighs deeply.

FEDYA (*voice-over*): 'There are moments when I could
gladly strangle her, when, if I could . . .'

DOSTOYEVSKY'S STUDY. EVENING.
ANNA *is scribbling in shorthand.*

FEDYA (*voice-over*): '. . . stick a knife in her breast, I
would . . .'

BELL TOWER. DAY.
ALEXEI *stands alone.*

FEDYA (*voice-over*): '. . . I hate her.'

DOSTOYEVSKY'S STUDY. EVENING.
FEDYA *talks with a half-smile, his eyes closed, a cigarette in
his hand.*

FEDYA: 'But now I have a commission from her. I must
win at roulette.'

CASINO. EVENING.
ALEXEI *walks towards the casino.*

FEDYA (*voice-over*): 'Yes, win at all costs.'

18

CASINO. EVENING.

ALEXEI *moves like a sleepwalker through the casino, which is ablaze with light, the clusters of people around the roulette wheels and baccarat tables resembling the rings of hell. All of humanity is here.* ALEXEI *watches a staidly dressed* MIDDLE-AGED WOMAN, *accompanied by a* DWARF. *The* WOMAN *places her bets coolly and calculatingly, taking notes with a pencil. Next to her a* YOUNG ARISTOCRAT, *dressed in impeccable evening clothes, places a large bet on black. Red turns up. Keeping his composure, the* YOUNG ARISTOCRAT *walks away from the table with a smile.*

CROUPIER: Faites vos jeux.

> ALEXEI *sits down in his seat. He takes some coins and looks around the table. Then he places a small bet on red.*

FEDYA (*voice-over*): 'My hands were shaking. The blood throbbing in my brain. I realised at that moment that I was a gambler.'

DOSTOYEVSKY'S STUDY. DAWN.

ANNA *is asleep in the chair.* FEDYA *makes a ghastly noise and she wakes with a start.* FEDYA *is weaving towards her, his face distorted.*

FEDYA: Polia! Polia!

> *He seizes her and pulls her to the floor as he falls.*

ANNA: It is I, Anna! Anna!

> FEDYA *howls like a beast, his eyes starting, foam frothing at his mouth. He trembles in the grip of an epileptic fit.* ANNA *doesn't know what to do: she's terrified.* USTINYA *runs in, taking in the situation quickly.*

USTINYA: He's taken a fit!

ANNA: What shall I do?

USTINYA: Hold his tongue! I'll fetch the doctor!

USTINYA *runs out.* FEDYA *writhes on the floor, now moaning incoherently.* ANNA *kneels over him and struggles to hold him still as she puts her hand in his foaming mouth. She is weeping with fear and misery.*

ANNA: I hate it here! I hate it here! I hate it!

DOSTOYEVSKY'S STUDY. DAY.
FEDYA *is lying on the couch, covered with a blanket.*

ANNA'S ROOM. DAY.
ANNA *has dressed in her outdoor clothes, and packed up her portfolio. She looks around the little room for the last time and leaves it.*

DOSTOYEVSKY'S STUDY. DAY.
ANNA *enters the study, holding a sheaf of papers. She stops as she sees* PASHA *at* FEDYA'*s desk. He stealthily opens the top drawer and takes out* FEDYA'*s wallet. He leafs through the banknotes inside and helps himself to a few. He looks up at* ANNA, *blows her a kiss and leaves quietly.* FEDYA *looks up at her from the couch.* ANNA *lays her papers on the desk, and plucks up her courage to speak.*

ANNA: I have prepared a fair copy of your manuscript. Mr Dostoyevsky, I am sorry to tell you this when you are unwell but I have decided that I am unsuited to this work. Or rather, that I am not compatible with my employer. I have never in my life been treated in this way, and I am a good stenographer.

FEDYA: Yes, you are.

ANNA: So I will return to my studies. I wish you a quick recovery. Good day.

She lays the manuscript on the top of a cabinet and leaves.

ANNA'S HOUSE. DAY.
Early morning. ANNA *walks towards the front door. She pushes it open.*

ANNA'S HOUSE. DAY.
ANNA *comes into the hallway, and stops outside her parents' bedroom. She sees the* DOCTOR *folding the arms of her dead* FATHER *across his chest, and closing his eyes. Her* MOTHER *weeps at the bedside. An* ORTHODOX PRIEST *stands near by, praying.*

DOCTOR: I am very sorry.
> ANNA'S MOTHER *wails over the body. The* DOCTOR *turns to* ANNA.
DOCTOR: Have you enough to pay for the funeral?
ANNA: No.
MOTHER: Not a pauper's grave, please. It must be done properly, Anna.

ANNA'S HOUSE. DAY.
ANNA *leaves her house, dressed in black. She carries a suitcase.*

DOSTOYEVSKY'S APARTMENT. DAY.
ANNA *stands at the door. She looks pale and sad.*

ANNA: Good morning.

USTINYA: Come in.

DOSTOYEVSKY'S STUDY. DAY.
FEDYA *stands at the desk, checking his papers and writing. He looks up and notices* ANNA *at the door.*

FEDYA: Couldn't keep away, eh?
ANNA: Not exactly.
FEDYA: Curious to know how it ends?

    ANNA *begins to answer but she is interrupted by* USTINYA.

USTINYA: Mr Stellovsky is here.

    FEDYA *drops his pencil and his glasses on the desk. He looks up as* STELLOVSKY *enters. He's a large, voluptuous man in an extravagant fur cape. They shake hands.*

STELLOVSKY: Maestro.
FEDYA (*to* ANNA): Mr Stellovsky is my publisher – This is Miss Snitkina, my assistant.

    STELLOVSKY *kisses* ANNA's *hand.*

STELLOVSKY: My dear. (*Turning to* FEDYA.) Well, how is it going?

    FEDYA *indicates the small pile of papers on the desk.*

FEDYA: I have made a start, but I am very weak. I had an attack of epilepsy in the night. As usual, I remember nothing of it.
STELLOVSKY: How terrible for you. What brings it on?
FEDYA: I'm told it has something to do with drinking champagne. I went out with Maikov last night.
STELLOVSKY: To write a novel in twenty-seven days is difficult enough, Fyodor Mikhailovich, without getting drunk on champagne. Even with such a fetching assistant. (*To* ANNA.) You don't really think he can do it, do you, my dear? In twenty-seven days? I do hope he has paid you in advance.

22

FEDYA (*embarrassed*): She knows nothing of the contract.

STELLOVSKY: But that's unfair! To employ someone, when you haven't a hope of reimbursing them? Grossly unfair! I really think you ought to tell her.

FEDYA (*to* ANNA): One year ago, Mr Stellovsky bought the rights to all my works for three thousand roubles, a sum which was long ago swallowed up by my commitments to my family. But the contract contained an unusual clause: I agreed to provide my publisher with a new novel, of not less than one hundred and sixty pages, by the first of September this year.

STELLOVSKY: A year ago that was a perfectly reasonable deal.

FEDYA: If I fail to deliver by the appointed time, Stellovsky owns everything I shall ever write. Everything I'll ever write, for no further payment. And I signed this devil's covenant. God forgive me my stupidity! I was so deep in debt, I signed. (*Glancing at* ANNA.) That's why you are here. You're my last chance.

ANNA *looks at him with some sympathy.*

STELLOVSKY: I can be generous, you know. I could advance you, say, a thousand? – against the masterpieces of the future. (*He holds out money.*) Have a few days off. Rest.

ANNA (*blurts out*): It's not enough! Don't take it!

FEDYA *looks at her, surprised at her response.*

STELLOVSKY: Well, then work! Work, for a crust of bread and a mug of tea. I'm content.

ANNA: Sir, I do not understand how you can rejoice at another's misfortune.

STELLOVSKY: He is a magnet for misfortune; if he was happy, do you think he could write? (*Pointing at the pile of paper.*) What is this book to be called, maestro?

FEDYA: I will call it 'Roulettenburg'.

STELLOVSKY: Rot. Sounds foreign.

STELLOVSKY *walks past* ANNA *to the hallway.*

STELLOVSKY: Think of something else. (*To* ANNA.) Au revoir.

STELLOVSKY *leaves.* FEDYA *and* ANNA *look at each other in silence.*

ANNA: Can you pay me?

FEDYA: If we finish it. Do you want to gamble?

ROULETTENBURG, CASINO. EVENING.

The wheel spins. ALEXEI *watches it.*

CROUPIER (*voice-over*): Rien ne va plus.

The ball lands on 36 red.

CROUPIER (*voice-over*): Trente-six, rouge, pair et manque.

ALEXEI: Yes!

He leaves his money there. He wins.

CROUPIER (*voice-over*): Mesdames et messieurs, faites vos jeux. Rien ne va plus.

Through the crowd around the table, KARL, *the bellboy from the hotel, approaches* ALEXEI. *The wheel spins. The ball stops on 12 red.* ALEXEI*'s money is doubled.*

CROUPIER (*voice-over*): Douze, rouge, pair et manque.

On the balcony stands BLANCHE. *She is watching* ALEXEI.

CROUPIER (*voice-over*): Mesdames et messieurs, faites vos jeux.

ALEXEI *moves all his winnings on to 28.*

KARL: No, don't put it on a single number. You'll lose everything.

ALEXEI *is surprised by* KARL, *who holds his arm. He takes his advice, and moves the money on to black. The wheel spins. The ball stops on 11 black.*

ALEXEI: Yes!

ALEXEI *smiles. People applaud.*

GRAND HOTEL, SALON. DUSK.

The GENERAL'S PARTY *are amongst the* GUESTS *in a salon, where a chamber orchestra plays a syrupy waltz.* MADAME DE COMINGES *sits next to the* GENERAL.

MADAME DE COMINGES: Would you like to play canasta, General?

The GENERAL *puts down the newspaper he is reading.* POLINA *glances up from her card game to see* DE GRIEUX *watching her.*

CASINO. NIGHT.

ALEXEI *now has a moderately large pile of money, placed on black.* KARL *still stands by his side, encouraging him in a friendly way.*

CROUPIER (*voice-over*): Mesdames et messieurs, faites vos jeux. Rien ne va plus.

The ball stops on red 9.

CROUPIER (*voice-over*): Neuf, rouge, impair et manque.

The crowd groans.

KARL: Bad luck, my friend.

BLANCHE *leaves her place at the balcony.* ALEXEI *can't believe it as the* CROUPIER *takes the pile of money away from him.*

ALEXEI: No! No!

DOSTOYEVSKY'S STUDY. DUSK.

ANNA *sleeps at the desk, resting her head on her papers.*

GRAND HOTEL, CORRIDOR. DUSK.

POLINA *walks nervously along a corridor. She hears the*

sound of a man's heavy boots behind her. She walks on, quickening her step. The footsteps appear to follow her. She almost runs now, glancing over her shoulder with a mixture of fear and excitement.

GRAND HOTEL, POLINA'S ROOM. DUSK.
POLINA *arrives at the door to her bedroom, opens it and steps inside.* DE GRIEUX *is there in the half-dark. He has his foot up against the bedstead, and is holding something soft and lacy, taken from an open drawer. He looks up at* POLINA, *victoriously. She gasps, and flattens herself against the wall.* DE GRIEUX *holds the article of underwear to his cheek, luxuriating in its feel.* POLINA *holds out her hand for it.* DE GRIEUX *pushes her back and tries to kiss her, but she turns her head away. He smiles, places the stocking in her hand, and leaves the room.*

DOSTOYEVSKY'S APARTMENT, DINING-ROOM. NIGHT.
FEDYA *and* ANNA *eat. A third place is empty.*

ANNA: She is fascinating. Strange, and dangerous . . . and vulnerable, too. What an imagination you have!
   FEDYA *looks oddly at her, but doesn't respond to the compliment.*
FEDYA: And Alexei?
ANNA (*thoughtfully*): I like him; but I worry that he is weak . . . that he will squander his life at the roulette table.
FEDYA (*smiles*): Maybe he will win.
ANNA: But he cannot control himself.
FEDYA (*earnestly*): Oh, I assure you, it's entirely possible to be possessed of an iron will, and yet lack the strength to resist the lure of roulette.
   Hearing his tone, ANNA *looks at him with a dawning suspicion.*

26

ANNA: Is Alexei familiar to you, Mr Dostoyevsky?

FEDYA: I write fiction, Miss Snitkina.

They are interrupted by PASHA *entering the dining-room. He is exquisitely dressed.*

FEDYA: Where have you been, Pasha?

PASHA: I paid a visit to my aunt and to my cousins, Papa. They say that they have had no money from you for a month. They are very angry, Papa. Don't you think you ought to send a little something? Say, a hundred roubles?

FEDYA (*mutters*): Oh, God, will it never end?

FEDYA *disappears into his study.* ANNA *is left alone with* PASHA.

ANNA: May I ask you something?

PASHA: You may, because you are pretty. Were you ugly, I should ignore you.

He looks down his nose at her. ANNA *finds his manner offensive, but perseveres.*

ANNA: Why was your father sent to prison?

PASHA (*laughs*): Oh, that old tale of woe. Every girl who fancies him must hear it.

ANNA: I do not 'fancy him'.

PASHA: No? No, of course not. You're a sensible girl. You wear sensible shoes. But deep inside, you long to taste all that is forbidden.

ANNA: I don't know what you're talking about.

PASHA: It's amazing, the success he has with students. Maybe I should rip up my clothes, hmm? Tear out my hair? Have an epileptic fit? Would you sleep with me then?

ANNA *slaps his face.*

DOSTOYEVSKY'S STUDY. NIGHT.

ANNA *enters the study.* FEDYA *is on his knees, praying before an icon. A battered copy of the New Testament is open in his hands.* ANNA *makes to leave again.*

FEDYA: No – pray with me.

    ANNA *kneels next to him on the floor.*

FEDYA: This New Testament came from Tobolsk, gateway to Siberia. It came from the wives of the Decembrist revolutionaries, men who'd been imprisoned there twenty-five years before. These innocent women had followed their husbands into exile, abandoned every comfort just to be with them. They told us not to lose courage, not to lose the will to survive, as we travelled through the snow to the house of the dead. And in the binding of this Bible, here, I found a ten-rouble note.

    He takes her hand and prays. They look up at the icon.

FEDYA: Almighty God, we pray for the salvation of the common people, and for the salvation of Russia, for the two are one and the same. Let their chains be broken, their eyes be lifted up, in the service of the Lord. Let there be a great renewal, springing from the soil, from the hands and hearts of the peasants! Merciful Father, we offer our lives and our work for You, in gratitude for the sacrifice of Your only Son, Jesus Christ our Lord. Amen.

ANNA: Amen.

    ANNA *looks at* FEDYA *with, for the first time, a sneaking admiration. He has revealed a side of himself that has hitherto been hidden. He has a mission. She finds this attractive.*

ANNA: You must have suffered terribly.

FEDYA (*suddenly brusque again*): It did me no harm.

ANNA: But surely—

FEDYA: No. I was guilty, and I was punished. It is just. I

28

refuse to complain. It made me a better Christian and a better writer. Come, let us work.

ROULETTENBURG, CASINO. DAWN.
ALEXEI *leaves the casino, shattered.*

GRAND HOTEL, ROOM OF MIRRORS. DAWN.
In a disused room with huge gilt mirrors on all four walls, and very little furniture except a couple of broken chairs, POLINA *lies on a couch.*

GRAND HOTEL. DAWN.
ALEXEI *walks towards the rear entrance of the Grand Hotel. He stumbles a little.*

ROOM OF MIRRORS. DAWN.
POLINA *sleeps on the couch.* ALEXEI *enters the room. He stands by her. After a while she wakes.*

ALEXEI: Polina.
She looks up at him, sees his forlorn expression, and immediately knows what has happened.
POLINA: You lost?
ALEXEI *nods.* POLINA *shuts her eyes.*
POLINA: Then I am lost too.
ALEXEI *sinks to the floor and puts his arms around* POLINA*'s legs. She clutches at him. They hold each other tight.*

DOSTOYEVSKY'S STUDY. NIGHT.

ANNA *is sitting with her arms bent over papers.* FEDYA *smokes, unhappily.*

ANNA: What's the matter?

FEDYA: There's no point in this. We will lose. Whatever happens, we will lose.

ANNA: You must work. We can do it.

GRAND HOTEL, GENERAL'S SUITE. DAY.

ALEXEI *knocks at the door of the salon.*

GENERAL (*voice-over*): Enter.

POLINA *is sitting by the window. The* GENERAL *rises from behind a table laden with food.* BLANCHE *and* MADAME DE COMINGES *sit either side of him.* DE GRIEUX *stands by the other window. They all look sternly at* ALEXEI.

GENERAL: It has come to my attention that you have wasted large sums of money at the casino.

ALEXEI: It's not true.

BLANCHE: Oh, but I saw you there, little one. I saw you lose at roulette!

DE GRIEUX: Was it your own money?

POLINA *glances at* ALEXEI. ALEXEI *catches her look.*

ALEXEI: Yes, of course.

GENERAL: And how did you acquire so much?

ALEXEI: Well, I started off with very little, from my own pocket, and it grew, and grew – and then in one spin of the wheel I lost the lot.

DE GRIEUX: This confirms my point: roulette is the ruin of Russians. (*Laughter from the company. To* ALEXEI.) You play with such hot temper, you invariably lose.

ALEXEI: Whereas the French invariably win, because they cheat.

DE GRIEUX: Monsieur!

There is general consternation. POLINA *watches* ALEXEI *closely.*

GENERAL: This is intolerable! – Sir, as you are my children's tutor, I must require you to stay away from the gaming tables. If you lose, I shall be compromised. And if you win a fortune, then, too, I shall be compromised.

DOSTOYEVSKY'S STUDY. DAY.
The clock strikes three. FEDYA *is working.* ANNA *stands to leave.*

ANNA: Excuse me, but I have to go out.

FEDYA: Out? No, I cannot allow it.

ANNA: I'm sorry, but I must go.

FEDYA: No, no, we have work to do. What can be more important than work?

ANNA: My father's funeral.

ANNA'S HOUSE. DAY.
ANNA, *her* MOTHER, IVAN *and* DUNYA *are attending the funeral service for* ANNA's FATHER. *The* PRIEST *swings the censer and spreads incense. A* CHOIR *sings a hymn.*

ST PETERSBURG, MARKET. DAY.
IVAN *walks* ANNA *back to Dostoyevsky's house.*

IVAN: It was a fine service.

ANNA: Yes, it was. Thank you for the money. I will pay you back.

IVAN: How is your work?

ANNA: It's hard.

IVAN: What's he like, this Dostoyevsky?

ANNA: He is . . . unusual.

IVAN: Handsome?

ANNA (*laughs*): No. Not like you.

IVAN: But talented.

ANNA: Very.

IVAN: What's the story about? Not filthy, I hope?

ANNA: It gets a little steamy in parts. (IVAN *looks alarmed.*)
There's nothing to worry about though, Ivan.

IVAN: Be careful, Anna. We have files on him at the
Ministry. Promise me, when this is over, you'll come
back.

*ANNA wants to kiss him, but he leans away. Then he
relents and gives her a quick peck on her cheek.*

DOSTOYEVSKY'S APARTMENT. DAY.

*ANNA enters the apartment. She sees PASHA sitting, dressed in
his Arabian robes. He's drinking vodka.*

PASHA: You look like you need a drink.

*ANNA nods. He pours her a glass and she downs it in
one gulp.*

PASHA: Would you permit me to show you my room?

*ANNA is curious. PASHA shows her into his bedroom and
closes the door behind them.*

PASHA'S ROOM. NIGHT.

*ANNA gazes about her in disbelief. PASHA's room is decorated
like a Persian brothel. Awnings hang from the ceiling like a
tent. There are tapestries on the walls, and burning incense in
carved ivory holders. His bed is a huge canopied affair.*

PASHA *sits cross-legged on the bed, puffing a pipe of opium.*

PASHA: Papa and his brother Mikhail were in some radical group, don't ask the name of it. They wanted a new Russia or something. (*He laughs at the idea.*) New Russia! All shit to me. Anyway, they got caught, and Papa was sentenced to be executed.

ANNA (*alarmed*): Executed?

PASHA: Yes, by order of the Tsar! They marched him in front of a firing squad. Put a hood over his head. Aimed their rifles and then – well, then they gave him a reprieve! (*He laughs.*) Just the Tsar's little joke. And when he came back to Petersburg, he brought with him a pile of manuscripts, a faith in God, and my mother, and me. Do you want to see the hood?

PASHA *takes the hood, puts it on his head and stumbles, laughing, to* ANNA. *He takes it off and hands it to her.*

ANNA: So you are not his real son?

PASHA: Oh, no. His stepson. Not the same blood. More vigorous.

He takes her hand and kisses it.

PASHA: More manly.

He continues kissing up her arm.

ANNA: Pasha, stop.

PASHA: Why?

He grabs her. Just then FEDYA *comes through the door, and finds the two of them apparently locked in an embrace on the bed.*

PASHA: You want to find out.

ANNA *throws off* PASHA.

ANNA: Pasha, no!

FEDYA: Pardon.

They look up at FEDYA, *who leaves hastily.*

PASHA: What's the matter, Papa – are you jealous?

ANNA *quickly follows* FEDYA.

DOSTOYEVSKY'S STUDY. EVENING.

ANNA *enters the study.* FEDYA *is lighting a cigarette.*

ANNA: I am sorry I made you angry.

FEDYA: What makes you think you made me angry?

ANNA: Please . . . I don't want you to misunderstand.

FEDYA *gestures to the desk.*

FEDYA: Back to work!

ANNA *takes her notebook and sits.*

FEDYA: How old are you?

ANNA: I'm twenty.

FEDYA: Are you in love with him?

ANNA *is taken aback.*

FEDYA: Write! 'Are you in love with him, Polina?'

GRAND HOTEL, ROOM OF MIRRORS. DAY.

ALEXEI *and* POLINA *are in the room of mirrors.*

POLINA: Love? What is love?

ALEXEI: Well, it's not all moonlight and roses, I can tell you.

POLINA: Are you jealous, Alexei?

ALEXEI: Only if you give me reason to be.

POLINA: Well, why should I give you reason for anything? What I think of De Grieux is my business. However, it is true that my stepfather has mortgaged all our property to him. Unless Grandmother dies soon, we will lose everything.

ALEXEI: So that is why they keep sending telegram after telegram asking if she's dead.

He laughs.

POLINA: It's not funny. Why are you so cheerful? Because you lost all my money?

ALEXEI: The money you gave me to lose. I was obeying

your orders, so don't blame me for the consequences. One day I'll gamble for myself and then I'll win. And then you can have whatever you need. When I'm rich you'll see me differently.

She laughs.

POLINA: Will I?

DOSTOYEVSKY'S STUDY. NIGHT.
ANNA *is writing.*

ALEXEI (*voice-over*): You're a heartless bitch.

POLINA (*voice-over*): Yes, but you love it, don't you?

ALEXEI (*voice-over*): Oh yes, I love it.

FEDYA (*voice-over, as* ALEXEI *throughout*): 'Wherever I go, whatever I do, I see your face before my eyes. It is an obsession. But I know I have no hope.'

FEDYA *is leaning over* ANNA's *shoulder as they read back the continuation of this scene from her notes. The experience affects them both:* FEDYA *is sweating and wringing his hands, in a tortuous ecstasy;* ANNA's *breast is heaving. There is an atmosphere of sexual excitement, which neither of them can ignore.*

ANNA (*as* POLINA *throughout*): 'Yet you think when you are rich you will be able to buy me.'

FEDYA: 'I never said that!'

ANNA: 'Oh, yes, you did.'

FEDYA: 'Polina, it is dangerous for you to be with me. One day I will kill you.'

ANNA: 'You really are jealous.'

FEDYA: 'Of course I am. Your coldness drives me into a frenzy. I want to hit you, beat you up, smash your face. And one day I will strangle you. – Don't laugh at me!'

ANNA: 'I'm not laughing! You're insane!'

ANNA'S ROOM. NIGHT.

ANNA *is asleep. The wind howls outside.*

FEDYA (*voice-over*): 'Every day I love you more!'
ANNA (*voice-over*): 'I order you to be silent!'

DOSTOYEVSKY'S STUDY. DAY.

ANNA *is seated at the desk.*

FEDYA: Shall we go back to work? Next chapter.

GRAND HOTEL, FOYER. DAY.

GRANDMOTHER *is sitting in a wheelchair. She's a little old
lady with remarkable eyesight and a powerful voice, who
appears distinctly un-dead. Her chamberlain* POTAPYCH,
*dressed in a frock coat and white waistcoat, assists her. A vast
collection of cases and portmanteaux is piling up on the ground
as the* FLUNKEYS *unload her carriage.*

GRANDMOTHER: Potapych. Get the manager!

DOSTOYEVSKY'S STUDY. NIGHT.

ANNA *dips her pen into the ink pot.*

GRAND HOTEL, FOYER. DAY.

GRANDMOTHER: Be careful, you flunkey! It's valuable!

GRAND HOTEL, STAIRCASE. DAY.

GRANDMOTHER *is being carried up the stairs in her*

wheelchair by FLUNKEYS. ALEXEI *runs up to her and kisses her hand.*

ALEXEI: Grandmother – what a surprise.

GRANDMOTHER: Alexei! Alexei Ivanovich! Oh! Where's that scoundrel son of mine?

ALEXEI: The General's party are on the first floor.

GRANDMOTHER: Does he have a decent suite?

GENERAL'S SUITE. DAY.

The door is flung open by POLINA, *and* GRANDMOTHER *is wheeled in by* ALEXEI. *A catastrophe. The* GENERAL, DE GRIEUX, BLANCHE *and* MADAME DE COMINGES *wear expensive riding habits;* DE GRIEUX *has on his high boots with spurs, and* BLANCHE *is once again in a low-cut outfit. She holds a whip. Her mouth falls open, the* GENERAL *gives a whimper of fear, and* DE GRIEUX *has a furious frown. They are so stunned that nobody moves.*

GRANDMOTHER: You expected a telegram. Well, here I am.

The GENERAL *hurries to kneel by the wheelchair and kiss his mother's hand.*

GENERAL: Dearest Mother – how on earth did you get here?

GRANDMOTHER: I caught a train, of course. How did you get here? By magic carpet? – Those cables must have cost you a great deal of money. I thought I'd save you that expense. You see, they have not nailed me into a box yet. I take it this is the Frenchman that you spend all your time with?

GENERAL: Allow me to present the Marquis de Grieux.

DE GRIEUX *forces himself to bow.* ALEXEI *is loving every minute of it.*

DE GRIEUX (*through clenched teeth*): Je suis enchanté,
   madame. Votre santé – c'est un miracle!
GRANDMOTHER: Très bien. (*To* BLANCHE.) Who are you?
GENERAL: This is Mademoiselle de Cominges. And this is
   her mother, Madame Veuve de Cominges.
BLANCHE (*curtseying*): Bonjour, madame.
GRANDMOTHER: You are very demure. Maybe you're an
   actress.
DE GRIEUX: But was your journey prudent, madame, for
   one of your years?
GRANDMOTHER (*to* ALEXEI): What did he say?
ALEXEI: He thinks you are too old to travel, Grandmother.
GRANDMOTHER: Monsieur, this trip has totally revived me.
   I feel ten years younger.
   DE GRIEUX *and the* GENERAL *look at each other in
   horror.*
GRANDMOTHER: Well, I hope I came in time to prevent
   my high-living son frittering away his last few roubles
   at roulette.
GENERAL: I don't play roulette, Mother.
GRANDMOTHER: Of course you play roulette. You play
   roulette and you lose. That's why you hocked
   everything to that Frenchman. I know everything. And
   I am determined to find out what it is about gambling
   that is so fascinating you can't tear yourself away from
   it. Alexei, where is that casino?
ALEXEI: It's just across the park, Grandmother.
GRANDMOTHER: All right. Let's go!

CASINO. DAY.
GRANDMOTHER's PARTY *enters the casino. She stares around
with great curiosity.*

GRANDMOTHER: Alexei, all these people, are they all
   playing?

ALEXEI *nods.* GRANDMOTHER *is carried down the stairs to the gambling floor.*

ALEXEI: We'll start with the roulette?

GRANDMOTHER: There are so many people. So much money, Alexei! (*Pointing at the spinning wheel.*) What is that?

DE GRIEUX, *the* GENERAL *and* BLANCHE *follow behind.*

DE GRIEUX: What shall we do?

GENERAL: What can we do?

DE GRIEUX (*despairingly*): Elle est sénile, tombée en enfance!

DOSTOYEVSKY'S STUDY. DAY.

ANNA *is animated.*

ANNA (*pleadingly*): But surely she won't lose everything!

FEDYA: Why not? The wheel is a great leveller.

ANNA: But there's no reason to it!

FEDYA: This is about obsession. In the grip of obsession, reason is suspended.

ANNA: I think you just like things to end badly.

FEDYA: I write from experience.

ANNA: I thought you said you made it up!

FEDYA: Ah.

He takes a cigarette and ANNA *lights it.*

CASINO. NIGHT.

GRANDMOTHER *is at a roulette table.* ALEXEI *is at her side.* POTAPYCH *stands behind her. The rest of the* GENERAL'*s* PARTY *hang back, watching from a distance.* GRANDMOTHER *watches the* GAMBLERS *with interest as they stake their bets and make their calculations.*

GRANDMOTHER: So that's rouge, and that's noir, and that's pair, that's impair – and what's he scribbling?

ALEXEI: He is trying to calculate the odds. See, he'll have a mathematical system to determine how to bet. Watch him.

They observe an aristocratic ENGLISHMAN, *who now stakes a large sum of money. The wheel spins; the ball drops on to zero.*

CROUPIER: Zéro!

GRANDMOTHER: What happened? Has he won?

ALEXEI: No, no, he has lost. Everybody loses on zero.

They watch another coup. GRANDMOTHER *is fascinated.*

CROUPIER: Mesdames et messieurs, faites vos jeux!

GRANDMOTHER: What's zero?

ALEXEI: Zero is when the bank wins. When the wheel stops on zero, everything on the table goes to the bank. Unless you have deliberately staked zero. In that case, you'll win thirty-five times your money back.

GRANDMOTHER: Thirty-five times your money back! Why don't these people bet on that?

ALEXEI: Because the odds against it turning up are thirty-six to one.

GRANDMOTHER: Oh, nonsense! It just came up! Potapych, where's my money?

POTAPYCH: Here, madam.

POTAPYCH *hands her a purse.* GRANDMOTHER *rummages in it, takes out a very small coin, and gives it to* ALEXEI.

GRANDMOTHER: Put that on zero.

ALEXEI: With respect, Grandmother, you will lose. Zero never turns up twice in a row. It might not come again tonight!

GRANDMOTHER: Do as I say.

CROUPIER: Faites vos jeux! Rien ne va plus!

ALEXEI *stakes on zero.* GRANDMOTHER *watches the*

spinning wheel like a cat looking at a bird. The wheel spins and the ball lands on 31 black.

CROUPIER: Trente et un, noir, impair et manque.

She loses. She immediately takes out another small coin.

GRANDMOTHER: Again. Zero.

ALEXEI: No, you cannot do that. Grandmother, perhaps we had better go.

GRANDMOTHER: You know what will happen the minute we stop? That wretched zero will turn up! Come on now, put on a couple this time, on zero.

ALEXEI: On zero?

GRANDMOTHER: On zero! Zero! Zero, zero!

CROUPIER: Mesdames et messieurs, faites vos jeux!

ALEXEI *bets two gold coins.*

CROUPIER: Rien ne va plus.

As the wheel spins, GRANDMOTHER *is almost trying to haul herself out of her chair, so great is her excitement.*

CROUPIER: Zéro!

ALEXEI: Yes!

GRANDMOTHER: We have won! How much do we get?

A CROUPIER *pushes two large packets of gold coins towards her with his rake.* ALEXEI *shares in the old lady's excitement.*

ALEXEI: It's incredible! Twice in a row. I've never seen that before!

POTAPYCH: The hotel, madam?

GRANDMOTHER: No! No! Quickly, do it again before that man spins that thing again! Come on, zero, zero!

ALEXEI: Grandmother, you'll lose!

GRANDMOTHER: Heaven is with me! Come on, the maximum! Zero!

She gives ALEXEI *her purse. He puts the maximum stake on zero. The wheel spins.*

CROUPIER: Mesdames et messieurs, faites vos jeux. Rien ne va plus. Cinq, rouge, impair et manque.

They lose. The GENERAL, BLANCHE *and* DE GRIEUX
are watching from the side.

GENERAL: She has lost her mind.

DE GRIEUX: Oui – tombée en enfance!

BLANCHE *gives the* GENERAL *a look which says: If she
loses everything, you can forget it.* GRANDMOTHER *seems
possessed by a kind of fury.*

GRANDMOTHER: Put on as much as we can! Zero, zero!

A crowd has gathered to watch the crazy old woman.

ALEXEI *places the bet.*

CROUPIER: Faites vos jeux, mesdames et messieurs!

The wheel spins . . .

CROUPIER: Rien ne va plus . . .

and comes up on:

CROUPIER: Zéro!

GRANDMOTHER: Ah!

GRANDMOTHER *sinks back in her chair, exhausted.
There is a cheer from the crowd as a vast pile of money is
pushed towards her.* ALEXEI *watches her with admiration.*
BLANCHE *embraces the* GENERAL. *The* GENERAL *pushes*
ALEXEI *aside and kneels to help* GRANDMOTHER *collect
the coins. He takes some and she notices. She slaps his
face, then embraces him.*

HANGER-ON: Give me a hundred and I'll make it a
thousand!

More and more people crowd around GRANDMOTHER,
flattering and begging in different languages. A close-up of
ALEXEI, *dreaming of success at the tables.*

DOSTOYEVSKY'S STUDY. DUSK.

FEDYA, *tired, is lying on the couch.* ANNA *finishes writing.*

FEDYA: Full stop.

ANNA: Is Alexei becoming addicted to roulette?

FEDYA: It happens to people.

ANNA: Well, can't we save him?

FEDYA: 'Save him'? Anna, I don't know what kind of books you normally read, but I write about life. Anyway, why should it matter to you whether he gambles or whether he doesn't?

ANNA: Then there is hope?

FEDYA: If there is faith.

ANNA: Then there is hope.

GRAND HOTEL, GRANDMOTHER'S SUITE. DUSK.

GRANDMOTHER, *looking drained from all the excitement at the casino, has been laid down to rest on a chaise longue. She motions to* ALEXEI. *He kneels at her side. A wizened old hand appears from under the blanket, and gives him a packet of gold coins.*

GRANDMOTHER: Alexei, take this. It's yours.

ALEXEI: Thank you.

GRANDMOTHER: Polina.

POLINA *is sitting at her other side.*

POLINA: Yes, Grandmother?

GRANDMOTHER: Polina, come with me to Moscow. I have an apartment in my house. It's yours. You are too good for this rat hole.

ALEXEI *watches* POLINA *closely to see how she will respond.*

POLINA: Your offer is very kind. But I cannot leave Roulettenburg, not now . . .

GRANDMOTHER *sighs, and sinks back on the chaise longue.*

GRANDMOTHER: May God be with you.

GRANDMOTHER *shuts her eyes and sighs deeply. In a few moments she is asleep.* ALEXEI *and* POLINA *look searchingly at each other.*

GRAND HOTEL, CORRIDOR. DUSK.

The GENERAL *and* DE GRIEUX *are in heated debate as they walk along the corridor. Behind them come* BLANCHE *and* MADAME DE COMINGES. *All are still wearing their riding clothes from the morning's interrupted outing.*

DE GRIEUX: You had better make sure you have something left to inherit, General.

GENERAL: Everything is under control, I assure you. My mother is returning to Moscow.

BLANCHE: The sooner the better.

DE GRIEUX: You put her on the train personally!

GENERAL: If you insist.

DE GRIEUX (*to the* LADIES): You stay here!

GRANDMOTHER'S SUITE. DUSK.

The GENERAL *and* DE GRIEUX *enter* GRANDMOTHER*'s suite.* GRANDMOTHER *sleeps on the chaise longue.* ALEXEI *and* POLINA *stand behind her.*

ALEXEI: Shh!

POLINA: She wants to go back to Moscow.

The GENERAL *turns to* DE GRIEUX *with relief.*

GENERAL: There. You see? You will get your money back. We Russians are not as feckless as you assume.

At that moment GRANDMOTHER *suddenly sits bolt upright, wide awake, eyes gleaming with enthusiasm.*

GRANDMOTHER: The casino! I want to go back!

DOSTOYEVSKY'S STUDY. NIGHT.

ANNA*'s reaction:*

ANNA: No!

44

CASINO. NIGHT.

GRANDMOTHER *has been at the roulette table for some time.*
ALEXEI *is at her side,* POTAPYCH *behind her, passing money.*
DE GRIEUX, BLANCHE, *the* GENERAL *and* POLINA *watch
with anguished expressions.* GRANDMOTHER *is losing heavily.*

GENERAL: Mother—

DE GRIEUX (*to* ALEXEI): Stop her!

ALEXEI: How?

GRANDMOTHER: How much have I lost? – It doesn't
matter. There is more. Put it all on zero.

ALEXEI: It might never turn up! Grandmother, I implore
you, please bet with more consideration for the odds.
Then we might have a chance of winning!

GRANDMOTHER: Maybe you are right. Forget that
wretched zero. Put five thousand on seven, that is my
saint's day.

ALEXEI *makes the bet. He looks up to see* DE GRIEUX
whispering in POLINA's *ear. Then she slips away through
a side door.*

CROUPIER: Mesdames et messieurs, faites vos jeux.

DE GRIEUX *stays behind, watching. The wheel spins.*
ALEXEI *sighs.*

CROUPIER: Rien ne va plus. – Zéro!

The GENERAL *almost swoons. At first* GRANDMOTHER
*cannot quite comprehend what is happening as her five
thousand is raked away. Then she rounds on* ALEXEI,
seething.

GRANDMOTHER: Look what you've done! Why did I listen
to you?

BLANCHE *turns on her heel and leaves the* GENERAL's
side. She goes towards a handsome young ITALIAN *who
has been smiling at her.* ALEXEI *sees* DE GRIEUX *go out
through the same door as* POLINA.

ALEXEI: All I did was explain to you the laws of chance –

45

I'm not responsible if you lose!

GRANDMOTHER: You are bringing me bad luck! Go away. Leave me alone.

ALEXEI (*softly*): There are people here who will rob you—

GRANDMOTHER: Leave me alone. Go away!

ALEXEI leaves her side. GRANDMOTHER *sighs in despair.*

CROUPIER: Mesdames et messieurs, faites vos jeux!

The aristocratic ENGLISHMAN *who was previously at the table sidles up next to* GRANDMOTHER.

ENGLISHMAN: May I be of assistance, madam?

She looks up.

GRANDMOTHER: Yes! You can bet for me. Put everything on zero.

ENGLISHMAN: Of course, madam. Let me do it for you.

CROUPIER (*voice-over*): Merci. Mesdames et messieurs, fait vos jeux.

GRANDMOTHER *waits.*

CROUPIER (*voice-over*): Rien ne va plus.

She waits.

CROUPIER (*voice-over*): Douze, rouge, pair et manque.

Freeze on GRANDMOTHER's *anguished face as the full extent of her loss sinks in.*

CASINO, STOREROOM. NIGHT.

Kneeling on all fours on the green baize, quite naked, is POLINA. *Her head hangs over the roulette wheel, which is spinning, a ball jumping in the slots.* DE GRIEUX *kneels behind her, fully dressed, his boot-leather creaking as he fucks her. The roulette ball comes to a halt.*

POLINA: Seven.

DE GRIEUX *thrusts into her, counting out loud as he does so:*

DE GRIEUX: One, two, three . . .

DOSTOYEVSKY'S STUDY. NIGHT.
ANNA's *reaction: she's wearing an expression of shock.*

DE GRIEUX (*voice-over*): . . . four . . .

CASINO, STAIRWELL. NIGHT.
ALEXEI *descends the stairs.*

DE GRIEUX (*voice-over*): . . . five, six, seven!

CASINO, STOREROOM. NIGHT.
POLINA *looks up through her sweat and flopping hair, to catch the eye of* ALEXEI *who is peering through the drapes, fascinated, unable to tear himself away.* POLINA *doesn't break from his gaze.*

DE GRIEUX (*voice-over, brutishly*): Again!
    POLINA *spins the wheel and throws in the ball.*
POLINA (*voice-over*): Nine.
DE GRIEUX (*voice-over*): One, two, three, four, five, six, seven, eight, nine. Again.

DOSTOYEVSKY'S STUDY. NIGHT.
ANNA *and* FEDYA *sit across the room from one another. They stare into each other's eyes. A long, long pause – very tense.*

ANNA: Do you wish to make any corrections?
FEDYA: No.

GRAND HOTEL. NIGHT.
ALEXEI *returns to the hotel.*

47

ROOM OF MIRRORS. NIGHT.
ALEXEI *walks through the room.*

GRAND HOTEL, CORRIDOR. NIGHT.
The GENERAL *kisses* BLANCHE*'s hand in the doorway to her room.*

GENERAL: I love you, Blanche.
BLANCHE: Oh, but you lost, mon Général. Dommage.
    She closes the door in his face. He staggers away, crying like a child, without noticing ALEXEI *who passes him.*

GRAND HOTEL, LOBBY. NIGHT.
ALEXEI *sees* DE GRIEUX *in the lobby. He is dressed for travelling and talking with the* MANAGER. BELLBOYS *carry his luggage.*

DE GRIEUX: Bringen Sie das alles runter!
MANAGER: Es tut mir schrecklich leid, Herr Baron.
DE GRIEUX: Die Rechnung schicken Sie nach Frankfurt.
MANAGER: Gerne. Auf Wiedersehen. Gute Reise.

GRAND HOTEL, PORTICO. NIGHT.
DE GRIEUX *departs hastily from the hotel in a carriage.*

DOSTOYEVSKY'S APARTMENT. NIGHT.
FEDYA *walks up the stairs to* ANNA*'s room.*

GRAND HOTEL, STAIRWELL. NIGHT.
ALEXEI *walks up the stairs to his bedroom.*

DOSTOYEVSKY'S APARTMENT. NIGHT.
FEDYA *comes to* ANNA*'s room. He stops and turns the door handle.*

GRAND HOTEL, ALEXEI'S ROOM. NIGHT.
ALEXEI *reaches the door to his room and turns the hand. As he enters, he finds* POLINA *sitting on his little bed.*

POLINA: Light the candle.

DOSTOYEVSKY'S APARTMENT, ANNA'S ROOM. NIGHT.
The door of ANNA*'s tiny bedroom opens. She's sitting on the bed, unlacing her boots. She gives a little gasp of surprise as she sees* FEDYA *standing in the doorway, and leaps to her feet.*

FEDYA: I was just wondering if I could get you something? Anything you need. A glass of milk or something?
A pause as she stares at his face in the candlelight. He tries to smile.
ANNA: No. I'm fine.
FEDYA: About the book – I don't expect you to understand. Sometimes I barely do myself.
She nods.
FEDYA: Sorry. Good-night.
FEDYA *decides to retreat.*
ANNA: Good-night.
He leaves, closing the door softly behind him. ANNA *sits down on her bed. A moment later the door handle turns again.* FEDYA *enters the bedroom and locks the door behind him.*

ALEXEI'S ROOM. NIGHT.
ALEXEI *and* POLINA *embrace*.

POLINA: I need you.
> *He throws her on the bed.*

ALEXEI (*angry*): I saw you with him.

POLINA: Yes.

ALEXEI: With de Grieux.

POLINA: Yes.

ALEXEI: How was it?

POLINA: Stop it.
> *He walks to the table and picks up a piece of paper.*

ALEXEI: What's this?

POLINA: It's a railway ticket.

ALEXEI: You're leaving?

POLINA: He's gone to Frankfurt, to sell all the General's property.

ALEXEI: Good.

POLINA: He wants me to follow.

ALEXEI: Will you?
> *She shrugs.*

ALEXEI: You love him, don't you?

POLINA: I owe him fifty thousand francs.

ALEXEI: But you love him.

POLINA: That's why I asked you to gamble for me.

ALEXEI: So you could be free, you said.

POLINA: Yes.

ALEXEI: So you could give yourself to him freely?

POLINA: Yes. As freely as I come to you.

ANNA'S ROOM. NIGHT.
FEDYA *looks deep into* ANNA's *eyes. She returns the look. It's a very serious look, rich with sexual promise but at the same time tender and loving. He caresses her face and her hair. He kneels on the floor and continues the unlacing of her boot.*

DOSTOYEVSKY'S APARTMENT, COURTYARD. NIGHT.
A carriage arrives at the front door. Inside it sits a WOMAN
with a strong resemblance to POLINA.

ANNA'S ROOM. NIGHT.
FEDYA *kisses* ANNA'*s ankle.*

DOSTOYEVSKY'S APARTMENT. NIGHT.
Close-up: the WOMAN'*s hand, clad in an expensive glove,*
raps at the front door of the Dostoyevsky apartment.

DOSTOYEVSKY'S APARTMENT. NIGHT.
USTINYA, *dressed in her nightclothes and carrying a candle,*
grumpily opens the door. The WOMAN *enters the apartment.*

WOMAN: Mr Dostoyevsky, please.
USTINYA: Do you want me to wake him up?
WOMAN: Yes.

ANNA'S ROOM. NIGHT.
FEDYA *presses his cheek to* ANNA'*s little foot. She tentatively*
puts out her hand to touch his hair, but doesn't quite reach it
when . . . there is a sharp knock on the door. FEDYA *leaps to*
his feet. With a glance at ANNA, *he opens the door. Standing*
there is the WOMAN. *She is* APOLLINARIA SUSLOVA, *her*
hair pulled back to reveal a pair of drop ruby earrings,
sparkling in the light from the hallway. (She is played by the
same actress as POLINA, *but looking maybe ten years older.)*
She wears extravagant, bohemian clothes.

FEDYA: Polia!

51

SUSLOVA: Hello, Fedya.

> *Jolted by the sound of the name, her gaze fixed on the ruby earrings,* ANNA *is dazzled by* SUSLOVA'*s beauty.* SUSLOVA *catches sight of* ANNA *on the bed and looks at* FEDYA *with one eyebrow raised. Embarrassed, he makes an introduction.*

FEDYA: Apollinaria Suslova ... Anna Snitkina ... (*At a loss.*) She is helping me with a novel.

SUSLOVA (*smiles*): Yes, so I see ...

> FEDYA *leaves* ANNA *and goes to* SUSLOVA.

DOSTOYEVSKY'S APARTMENT, HALL. NIGHT.

SUSLOVA: How are you, Fedya?

FEDYA: How? Well, I'm fine, thank you.

> ANNA *watches him from above. They go into* FEDYA'*s study and he closes the door behind him.*

DOSTOYEVSKY'S STUDY. NIGHT.

SUSLOVA *and* FEDYA *look at each other intently.*

FEDYA: Polia, why are you here?

SUSLOVA: I heard you were ill.

DOSTOYEVSKY'S APARTMENT, HALL. NIGHT.

ANNA *stands outside the study door, listening.*

DOSTOYEVSKY'S STUDY. NIGHT.

SUSLOVA *comes to him and traces her fingers caressingly across his forehead and blotched cheeks.* FEDYA *closes his eyes at her touch.*

SUSLOVA: I can save you.

FEDYA: Save me?

SUSLOVA: From the demons ... You always said we were a matched pair. I'm going to Paris. Come with me. Remember how it was before? We'll wander on the boulevards, we will kiss on the bridges. And we will lie in bed listening to the bells. Money enough for three months. Come!

FEDYA: Paris!

FEDYA smiles at the memory. The door opens and ANNA bursts in.

ANNA: You cannot go to Paris! The deadline is in five days!

SUSLOVA: Leave your deadlines, leave your debts. Leave your Russian peasants to their mud and misery. Come to Paris. The train leaves at midnight.

ANNA: No!

FEDYA: Why do you torment me?

SUSLOVA: Because you like to suffer. Come with me. Be my slave. It will be delicious.

ANNA: I think you have said enough.

SUSLOVA: Fedya, you opened a door for me and I stepped through. And now I can never go back. The least you can do is come with me. And be my companion in hell.

ANNA: The pair of you are mad! This obsession with despair! What about all the good things? What about the decent people?

SUSLOVA: You have no idea what we're talking about, have you? Fedya, make up your mind!

FEDYA: I have a novel I have to write.

SUSLOVA: Well, write. Come on, write it! You've got all this moonlight and roses. Write about it! Write a love story, come on. Write a happy ending!

FEDYA: I can't bear this.

He runs from the room in agony.

DOSTOYEVSKY'S APARTMENT, COURTYARD. NIGHT.

ANNA *emerges into the dark courtyard. She arrives just in time to see* FEDYA *getting into a very luxurious carriage. She bangs on the door as it closes. With a crack of the whip, the carriage drives off.* ANNA *races behind for a few steps, but it's hopeless.*

ANNA: Fedya!

DOSTOYEVSKY'S STUDY. NIGHT.

SUSLOVA *is flicking through the pages of the manuscript; she reads the last page with a scornful expression as* ANNA *enters the study and confronts her.*

ANNA: Stellovsky brought you here. He knew what would happen.

SUSLOVA: Why, what has happened?

ANNA: Fyodor Mikhailovich has stopped work.

SUSLOVA *laughs. She holds up the manuscript.*

SUSLOVA: This is not work, it's a confession!

She starts to throw the pages around the room. They flutter like leaves in the air. ANNA *leaps towards her, but* SUSLOVA *skips away, laughing cruelly. The manuscript cascades around them.* ANNA *grabs at the paper.*

SUSLOVA *starts to tear the pages.*

ANNA: Don't do that! No! Don't do that!

SUSLOVA: Why not?

ANNA: I'll never know what happens.

ANNA *stares at the torn pages, aghast.*

SUSLOVA: Well, you know what he's like. What do you think happens?

CASINO. NIGHT.
A roar from the crowd of GAMBLERS. *A large pile of money is
pushed towards* ALEXEI, *who sits at the roulette table in
triumph.* KARL *stands next to him.* ALEXEI *is snapped out of
his reverie by the* CASINO MANAGER'*s voice. The game has
stopped.*

CASINO MANAGER: Monsieur, you have broken the bank.
    The table is closed.
    A large cloth is laid over the roulette table.

GRAND HOTEL, ALEXEI'S ROOM. NIGHT.
POLINA *is sitting on the bed with tears in her eyes, as*
ALEXEI *flings open the door. Without a word, he starts to
throw his money from a bag on to the bed and the floor.*

ALEXEI: Two hundred thousand francs!
    *He starts to grab the money again, obsessed with it,
    collecting a part of it in the bag. He holds the bag up to
    her.*
ALEXEI: Here's your fifty thousand. Go to Frankfurt
    tomorrow, and throw it in de Grieux's face.
    POLINA *looks him in the eye, and starts to laugh, the
    caustic laugh she has used on him so many times before.*
POLINA: It's too much. De Grieux's used lover is not
    worth fifty thousand francs. Not worth anything!
    Nobody wants me now!
ALEXEI: Well, I want you.
POLINA: Do you?
ALEXEI: Yes. I love you.
    He embraces her.

55

ALEXEI: I love you.

POLINA: Will you always?

ALEXEI: Yes, always.

POLINA: Let's run away together! (*They kiss.*) Let's go to
Italy! The train leaves at midnight!

POLINA *pushes him down on the bed, and straddles him.
Distant thunder is heard.*

DOSTOYEVSKY'S STUDY. NIGHT.

SUSLOVA *and* ANNA *sit on the floor amongst the piles of
scattered paper. They drink vodka. Outside, there is the sound
of a rising wind followed by a loud clap of thunder. There is a
great rush of air as the casement windows fly open.*

ANNA: Polina, help me!

*Both struggle together to force the windows shut, their
faces streaked with rain. With a final effort, they secure
the latch.*

DOSTOYEVSKY'S STUDY. NIGHT.

SUSLOVA *lies on the couch and looks at* ANNA, *sitting behind
the desk.*

SUSLOVA: Are you in love with him? Well, he's in love
with you. He must be, otherwise he would come to
Paris on his knees.

ANNA *struggles to take this in.*

SUSLOVA: If you go after him, nothing will ever be the
same again. The first thing you'll lose is your
innocence. The second, your hope.

ANNA: I'll never lose that.

SUSLOVA: Well, I lost mine.

GRAND HOTEL, ALEXEI'S ROOM. DAWN.
First light finds ALEXEI *waking up on a pile of bedclothes, half undressed.* POLINA *is sitting by the window, a strange look on her face.*

POLINA: Can I have my fifty thousand francs?
    Dazed, ALEXEI *stares at her.*
POLINA: My money. Can I have it?
ALEXEI: If you want.
POLINA: Wasn't I worth it? What about thirty?
    He goes to the table and empties the bag on to the table.
ALEXEI: There!
    She throws the coins back at him.
POLINA: If you loved me, you would not give it!
    She goes out quickly.

ST PETERSBURG, GAMBLING DEN. NIGHT.
The main action is a dice game in the centre of the cellar. It's dark and squalid. FEDYA *is at the heart of the crowd. Behind him stands* STELLOVSKY. ANNA *enters the gambling den.*

DICE PLAYER: Holy Mary, Mother of Christ,
                Save my soul and bless my dice.
    The dice are thrown. FEDYA *loses. He bets again.* ANNA
    watches impassively, apparently without judgement, as
    FEDYA *gambles. After losing,* FEDYA *leaves. He walks*
    past her without saying a word and she follows him.

ALLEYWAY. NIGHT.
ANNA *follows* FEDYA *out of the gambling den.*

FEDYA: You are angry with me?
ANNA: No.

57

FEDYA: Why not, for God's sake?

ANNA: You must do what you must do. I do not pretend to understand you. But you must finish your book or you'll never be able to hold your head up again.

FEDYA: So? I always lose.

ANNA: Please, come back to work.

FEDYA (*violently*): No! I cannot write! Not now! (*Gives her money.*) Here, take your fifty roubles and keep away from me. Stay away, you hear!

FEDYA throws the money at her. Then he turns and strides away from her. ANNA *stands in the alley, crying.*

STREET. NIGHT.
As FEDYA *rounds a corner he bumps into a* DRUNK. *The* DRUNK *curses, staggers and hits* FEDYA *hard.* FEDYA *falls against a pillar, cutting open his head.*

ST PETERSBURG. NIGHT.
ANNA *walks down a street in the pouring rain.*

ALLEYWAYS. NIGHT.
FEDYA *staggers through the poorly lit alleys, blood streaming down his face. He's dazed, despairing, almost a broken man.*

DOSTOYEVSKY'S APARTMENT BUILDING. NIGHT.
FEDYA *reaches his front door at the top of the stairs. Trying to open it, he collapses.* USTINYA *opens the door and he falls to the floor.*

USTINYA: Pasha, the doctor, quickly!

PASHA *steps over his father's body and turns to look at him.*

FEDYA (*muttering*): ... and the old woman, laughing, laughing ... and the axe comes down ... Terrible crime ... terrible!

PASHA *runs down the stairs.*

DOSTOYEVSKY'S STUDY. DAY.

FEDYA *is asleep on the couch. He wakes, and his eyes range around the room, taking in the now-substantial pile of manuscript paper on his desk. Something seems to be glinting strangely from within the papers. A peculiar light fills the room.* FEDYA *throws off his blanket and gets up to investigate. Going to the desk, he finds a diamond in among his papers. He holds it up to the light; it sparkles. He peers at it curiously.*

It's a dream. FEDYA *wakes again, on the couch. He walks over to his desk and looks over at the pile of papers: no diamond. He rubs his eyes; he can't figure it out. What does it mean?*

DOSTOYEVSKY'S STUDY. DAY.

Now recovered, FEDYA *attempts to work at his desk. First he tries to piece back together the papers that* SUSLOVA *tore up. It seems impossible. He puts them aside. Then he opens* ANNA's *notebook. He squints at it; he frowns. He can't decipher the shorthand.*

DOSTOYEVSKY'S APARTMENT, COURTYARD. DAY.

FEDYA, *without an overcoat, comes out of the house and runs into the street.*

59

ANNA'S HOUSE. DAY.

ANNA *sits in the parlour with* IVAN. *Her* MOTHER *brings in a samovar and tea glasses and then leaves them alone together, smiling.* ANNA *is restless.*

IVAN: Yes, I was promoted. (*Proudly.*) I have my own desk. Last Sunday after church I had quite an experience. I went to a restaurant! Have you ever been to a restaurant?

ANNA: No.

IVAN: Well, perhaps you may care to try, one day?

ANNA: Yes, thank you. That would be lovely.

A pause. A clock chimes quietly. ANNA *looks around her, suffocating in the silence, the inactivity of home. She turns back to see that* IVAN *has gone down on one knee.*

ANNA: Ivan—?

IVAN: It is possible that you have forgotten my proposal. So I will ask again.

He opens a jewellery box with an engagement ring in it, and holds it up to ANNA.

IVAN: Will you marry me, Anna?

ANNA (*looking at the ring*): It is beautiful.

IVAN: I know you think my life boring. But there's nothing wrong with a boring life. Many people lead one. Who are we to consider ourselves different?

ANNA: Dear Ivan. You are a good man. But don't you want to live just a little bit dangerously?

IVAN: No. I like order. I'm not some writer fellow with debts and a passion for gambling.

ANNA *is surprised that he knows so much.*

IVAN: He is under constant surveillance, you know. I've read his file at the Ministry. I am going up and up, Anna, I promise you.

ANNA *touches his hand.*

ANNA: Yes, I'm sure you are.

There is a violent knocking on the front door. ANNA
hurries out to the hallway, with IVAN *behind her, in time
to see her* MOTHER *admit* FEDYA. *He wears no overcoat,
and is drenched with rain. He looks terrible. He sees*
ANNA *and pushes past her* MOTHER.

FEDYA: Anna! Anna! I need you.

ANNA: Where is your coat? (*Seeing his wounds.*) What
   happened?

   FEDYA *sees* IVAN *standing behind* ANNA *with the
   engagement ring still in his hand.* FEDYA *looks crestfallen.*

FEDYA: I see you have company. I'm sorry.

   FEDYA *immediately leaves the house.* ANNA'S MOTHER
   closes the door firmly behind him. ANNA *turns to* IVAN,
   who has an imploring look.

ANNA'S HOUSE, ANNA'S BEDROOM. NIGHT.
ANNA *wakes in fright from a terrible dream.*

ANNA (*voice-over*): I hate it! I hate it!
   She sits up in her bed, shaking. She stands up.

DOSTOYEVSKY'S STUDY. DAWN.
ANNA *is sitting at the desk, transcribing her shorthand.*
FEDYA *is sleeping fitfully on his couch. He looks dishevelled.
In his sleep he hears a familiar sound: the scratch of pen on
paper.*

ANNA: Are you ready? Where were we?

FEDYA: I don't know.

ANNA: We have to work.

FEDYA: I am tired.
   He closes his eyes.

DOSTOYEVSKY'S APARTMENT, HALLWAY. DAY.

PASHA *is standing in his Arabian clothes opposite* ANNA. *He's not pleased.*

PASHA: So you're back. Where's the old boy?

ANNA: Your stepfather is sleeping.

PASHA: Asleep, for God's sake. We'll all starve.

ANNA: Isn't it about time you got a job? Who do you
think you are? The Tsar of all the Russias?
She walks out.

ANNA (*voice-over*): Ustinya, tea.

DOSTOYEVSKY'S APARTMENT. DAY.

ANNA *is at the front door. Two* CREDITORS *are on the doorstep, holding documents.* ANNA *fends them off.*

FIRST CREDITOR: We will take you to court!

ANNA: You can do whatever you like, but you're not
coming through this door. Good day.
She shuts the door firmly in their faces.

DOSTOYEVSKY'S STUDY. DAY.

ANNA: Where were we?

FEDYA: On our way to Paris.

DOSTOYEVSKY'S STUDY. NIGHT.

ANNA *is writing. She looks up at* FEDYA *who is asleep. She smiles.*

GRAND HOTEL, BLANCHE'S BEDROOM. DAY.

ALEXEI *is smartly dressed. The room is piled high with packed trunks, suitcases, hatboxes.* BLANCHE *is sitting on the edge of the bed, wearing fancy silk lingerie, and showing a lot of fine, tanned flesh.* ALEXEI *breathes deeply: she's gorgeous.* ALEXEI *has kneeled. He takes a silk stocking and slips it from her perfectly formed foot.*

BLANCHE: I heard you broke the bank last night, Alexei. I love a man who does that.
    As ALEXEI *rolls the stocking down over her calf, he bends and kisses her toes, caressing her ankle.*

BLANCHE: I am leaving for Paris in half an hour. You may come with me, if you wish. We will spend all your money in one month . . .

DOSTOYEVSKY'S STUDY. NIGHT.
ANNA *is writing.*

BLANCHE (*voice-over*): . . . You will live like you have never lived before. Ah, Paris.
    FEDYA *lies asleep on the couch.*

DOSTOYEVSKY'S APARTMENT, ANNA'S ROOM. DAY.
ANNA *is transcribing pages.*

ANNA (*voice-over*): Mr Stellovsky?

DOSTOYEVSKY'S STUDY. DAY.
ANNA *enters with the transcribed pages.* STELLOVSKY *is there, leafing through the pile of papers on the desk.*

STELLOVSKY: My dear, the maestro being asleep, I have

busied myself with a little stocktaking. (*Harshly.*) You work too fast. Too many pages. Go slower.

ANNA: I am supposed to go fast.

FEDYA *still lies asleep on the couch.*

ANNA'S ROOM. DAY.

ANNA *is transcribing pages.*

DOSTOYEVSKY'S STUDY. DAY.

ANNA *and* STELLOVSKY *stand in the doorway.*

ANNA: I have no intention of leaving.

STELLOVSKY *hands her his card.*

STELLOVSKY: I give this only to special lady friends. It's my place in the country.

DOSTOYEVSKY'S STUDY. DUSK.

ANNA *sits writing.*

DOSTOYEVSKY'S STUDY. DAWN.

ANNA *is asleep at the desk.*

FEDYA (*voice-over*): Good morning.

ANNA *wakes and yawns.*

DOSTOYEVSKY'S STUDY. DAY.

ANNA *looks up and frowns at the clock.*

ANNA (*voice-over*): Midnight tonight is the deadline and there is still much work to do.

DOSTOYEVSKY'S STUDY. DUSK.

ANNA *is writing.* FEDYA *is sleeping.* FEDYA *wakes.* ANNA
puts the last sheet on a pile of papers on her desk.

ANNA: Let's go!

ST PETERSBURG. NIGHT.
*A carriage races through the empty, dark, cobbled streets. The
weather is stormy, rain hammering against the windows.*

CARRIAGE. NIGHT.
Inside, being jolted around, are FEDYA *and* ANNA. *She is
clutching the manuscript and smiling at him.*

ST PETERSBURG. NIGHT.
*Long shots of the carriage as it passes through a smart district
of the city, intercut with* ANNA *and* FEDYA *completing the last
scenes of the novel in the study.*

ANNA: Where were we?
FEDYA: Grandmother has returned to Moscow . . .
ANNA: . . . Where she builds a new church for her
      peasants.
FEDYA: Of wood, not stone.
ANNA: Alexei and Blanche are in Paris . . .
FEDYA: . . . But they've run out of money.
ANNA: So . . . he returns to gambling. Where does he go?
FEDYA: Monte Carlo, Baden-Baden, every casino in the
      world.
ANNA: And he ends up in jail.
FEDYA: Does he?

ANNA: Yes, yes. And he suffers miserably . . . until . . .

FEDYA: Until he is rescued by Polina.

ANNA: Really?

FEDYA: Yes. He thinks so. He's not sure.

The carriage leaves the city. It drives through a forest.

ANNA: Never mind. He goes back to the tables and he wins and he loses and he wins . . .

FEDYA: You're getting the hang of this, aren't you?

ANNA: And Polina? Is she happy?

TRAIN. NIGHT.

SUSLOVA/POLINA *at the window of a train pulling out of a station. She is beautiful, and in despair.*

The carriage crashes onwards through the forest.

DOSTOYEVSKY'S STUDY. NIGHT.

ANNA *has finished the last lines of* FEDYA*'s manuscript. She wakes him. She thrusts a pen in his hand and smiles.*

ANNA: Sign it.

FEDYA, *still in a daze, takes his pen and signs the paper: 'Fyodor Mikhailovich Dostoyevsky, 1866.'*

Inside the carriage, ANNA *and* FEDYA.

STELLOVSKY'S COUNTRY HOUSE. NIGHT.

The carriage pulls up.

DOSTOYEVSKY'S STUDY. NIGHT.

ANNA: Time to go.

STELLOVSKY'S HALL. NIGHT.
A BUTLER *opens the door and* ANNA *steps in.*

ANNA: Mr Stellovsky, please.
BUTLER: He is not at home.
ANNA: But I have a private invitation.
She holds up STELLOVSKY*'s card. The* BUTLER *walks to a door and she follows. He knocks on the door.*

STELLOVSKY'S DINING-ROOM. NIGHT.
STELLOVSKY *is on a table, naked. He is being massaged by two buxom* COUNTRY GIRLS, *dressed in lingerie.*

BUTLER (*voice-over*): You have a visitor, sir!
STELLOVSKY: Entrez!
The BUTLER *lets* ANNA *in. She holds the manuscript behind her back.* STELLOVSKY*'s eyes widen as she enters the room.*
ANNA: Mr Stellovsky, I have decided to accept your invitation.
STELLOVSKY: Wonderful. Gown!
He stands up from the table, quickly putting on a dressing-gown and gestures the GIRLS *away.*
STELLOVSKY: Out. Out. (*To* ANNA.) Come in, Anna. Take off your cape.
He walks towards her.
ANNA: I have something very special to give you.
STELLOVSKY: I'm sure you do. Champagne?
ANNA: That won't be necessary. What I have to give you is this.
STELLOVSKY *frowns.*
STELLOVSKY: What?
ANNA *takes the manuscript from behind her back.*
ANNA: Fyodor Mikhailovich Dostoyevsky's novel.

67

ANNA *puts it on a table.*

STELLOVSKY'S COUNTRY HOUSE. NIGHT.
ANNA *runs out to* FEDYA, *standing at the carriage. They get in.* STELLOVSKY *comes out of the house, followed by his* BUTLER.

STELLOVSKY (*roaring*): It's not possible, in twenty-seven days! It's simply not possible!
FEDYA (*triumphantly*): It is possible Mr Stellovsky!
The carriage drives away into the mist.

COUNTRYSIDE. DAWN.
The carriage is parked under a tree in peaceful countryside. The horses graze nearby. ANNA *and* FEDYA *sit in the carriage as the sun rises. She sleeps with her head in his lap.* FEDYA *takes from his pocket a diamond ring (the one* ANNA *pawned at the start of the film) and slips it on her finger.*
    And cut to:

BADEN-BADEN, CASINO. DAY.
The casino, four years later. We pick up from the beginning of the story: close-up of ANNA, *searching for* FEDYA, *with worry etched into her face.* FEDYA, *in shabby clothes, sits at a roulette table.*

CROUPIER: Faites vos jeux.
FEDYA: Put it on zero.
    The wheel stops at black 35. ANNA *stands by his side with her* CHILD *in her arms.*
ANNA: Shall we go back to work?
    He looks up at her.

68

CASINO. DAY.

FEDYA, ANNA *and their* CHILD *leave the casino.*

BADEN-BADEN, STREET. DAY.

The down-at-heel FAMILY *walk away down a busy street.*

CAPTION: 'Dostoyevsky and his wife Anna roamed Europe
for four years, often in extreme poverty. During this
time he wrote *Crime and Punishment*, *The Idiot* and
The Devils. Anna took dictation.'

CAST

(in alphabetical order)

MAIKOV	Gijs Scholten van Asschat
MLLE BLANCHE	Angeline Ball
MME DE COMINGES	Marjon Brandsma
CROUPIER I	Ed de Bruin
MIDDLE-AGED WOMAN	Vittoria de Bruin
DUNYA	Lucy Davis
POTAPYCH	András Fekete
FYODOR DOSTOYEVSKY	Michael Gambon
CREDITOR	Zoltán Gera
PROFESSOR OHLKIN	Patrick Godfrey
USTINYA	Greet Groot
DWARF	Lajos István Hadjú
PASHA	William Houston
STELLOVSKY	Tom Jansen
MAN IN RAGS	Zoltán Kamondy
CASINO MANAGER	János Koltay
CREDITOR	Antal Konrád
IVAN	Mark Lacey
BUTLER	Antal Leisen
DE GRIEUX	Johan Leysen
SECRETARY	Nancy Manningham
ANNA SNITKINA	Jodhi May
HOTEL MANAGER	Károly Mécs
ENGLISH GENTLEMAN	Peter Meikle
HANGER ON	Michael Mehlmann
YOUNG ARISTOCRAT	András Mész
DOCTOR	Ferenc Némethi

GRANDMOTHER'S MAID	Éva Papp
PAWNBROKER	Géza Pártos
CROUPIER II	József Pilissy
GRANDMOTHER	Luise Rainer
ANNA'S FATHER	Miklós B. Székely
SHORTHAND PROFESSOR	Miklós Törkenczey
ANNA'S MOTHER	Vera Venczel
POLINA	Polly Walker
ALEXEI	Dominic West
THE GENERAL	John Wood
KARL	János Xantus

Director	Karoly Makk
Producers	Charles Cohen
	Marc Vlessing
Screenplay	Katharine Ogden & Charles Cohen and Nick Dear
Co-producer	Réne Seegers
Director of Photography	Jules van den Steenhoven NSC
Production Designer	Ben van Os
Casting	Celestia Fox
Music	Brian Lock
Costume Designer	Dien van Straalen
Editor	Kevin Whelan
Sound Designer	Wim Vonk
Line Producers	Karel van Ossenbrüggen
	Berry van Zwieten

First Assistant Director	Gábor Gajdos
Second Assistant Director	András Kécza
Third Assistant Director	Sylvia Pintér
Script Supervisor/Continuity	Sue Jones
Dialogue Supervisor	Nancy Manningham
Dutch Casting	Hans Kemna
Assistant Casting Director UK	Sophie Lane Fox

Sound Mixer	John Pitt
Boom Operator	Pál Szüros
Assistant Boom Operator	Szabolcs Stella
Focus Puller	Robbert van Dijk
Second Assistant Camera	Szilárd Makkos
Video Operator	Ákos Gulyás
Steadicam Operator	Luc Schengen
Still Photographer	Ferenc Markovics
	György Kalászi
Assistant Production Designer	Constance de Vos
Art Director	Lóránd Jávor
Second Art Director	Tibor Lázár
Supervising Make-up & Hair	Károly B. Temesvári
Key Make-up Artist	Edit Basilides
Hairstylist	István Szücs
Art Department Co-ordinator	Karin van der Werff
Set Decorator	István Töth
Flowers & Draperies	Ank van Straalen
Property Buyer	János P. Nagy
Property Master	Péter Gantner
On Set Dresser	Lívia Balogh
Props	Mihály Marton
Construction Co-ordinator	Lásló Nagy
Stand by Construction	E. Szabó Lajos
Assistant Costume Designer	Marie-Therese Jacobse
Wardrobe Master	György Homonnay
Wardrobe Assistant	Andrea Friebert
Costumers	Gyula Zámbó
	Gábor Simkó
	Mari Balázs-Piri
Gaffer	Béla Romwalter
Best Boy	József Szucsik
Electricians	Péter Bognár
	Pál Perlaki
	Tibor Molnár
	Ifj. György Garami

Key Grip	Pál Paluch
Grip	János Kiss
	Balázs Vákár
Generator Operator	Zsolt Büti
Swing Gang	Tamás Megyeri
	Ferenc Nagypál
	Zsolt Nemes
	József Ócsai
Special Effects	Ferenc Ormos
Stunt Co-ordinator	Béla Unger
Production Manager	Sàndor Baló
Unit/Location Manager	Tamás Maros
Unit/Location Manager	László Roráriusz
Production Co-ordinator	Tania C. Hammond-Adler
Hungarian Co-ordinator	Ágota Kovács
Key Production Assistant	Zsolt Csutak
Hungarian Co-ordinator	Agota Kovacs
Key Production Assistant	Zsolt Csutak
Production Secretary	Gabriella Csoma
Set P.A.	Bernadett Baló
Producer's Secretary UK	Katherine Anderson
	Shaheen Baig
	Laura Evans
Producer's Secretary NL	Monique van der Toom
Production Accountant	Wijgert Horst
Hungarian Production Accountant	Judit Kovács
Extra Co-ordinator	László Papp
Supervising Sound Editor	William Trent MPSE
Dialogue Editor	Piet Rodenburg
Assistant Editor	Gerrit Netten
Apprentice Editor	Henrik Meierkord
ADR Supervisor	Constantine Gregory
Foley Supervisor	Tony Message
Post Production Supervisors	Jeannete Healey
	Tania Windsor

74

Interpreters	Katalin Széphegyi
	Anna Szász
	Kati Baranayi
	Pálma Melis
	Judit Sági
	Kata Füstös
Freight Agent	Béla Frey
Fireman	Srankó Csaba
UK Transport Co-ordinator	Wallace Jacobs
Hungarian Transport Co-ordinator	László Lakatos
Drivers	István Varga
	András Greznevics
	Csaba Forgon
	András Grúz
	Béla Lakotos
	János Zeve
	András Filó
	József Rétfalusi
	János Molnár
	János Oravecz
	Ferenc Zilaja
	László Molnár
	János Schmál
	András Csáti
	Zoltán Varga
Medical Service	Oxy-Med BT.
Location Security	István Vanyó
Caterer	Géza Jánossy
Cleaning Lady	Farkas Rezscené Eta
AVID Facility NL	DGW Amsterdam
Mixing Facility UK	Anvil
ADR Facility UK	DB Post
Laboratory Services	Cineco Amsterdam
Color Timer	Pedro van Leeuwen
Negative Cutter	Romy de Haan

Opticals	Image Creations NL
Titles	Cine Image UK
Telecine	Valkieser NL
Production Bank	Guinness Mahon & Co
Bond Company	Film Finances
Insurance Company	Sampson & Allen
Legal Services	Westaway & Co

Music performed by City of Prague Philharmonic
Conducted by Stepan Konieck
Orchestrated by Brian Lock
Music Supervisor Ian Hierons
Music recorded at Smecky Studios, Prague
Recording Engineer Martin Astle
Music mixed at Ronnie Bond Studio, London
Music mixed by Martin Astle & Brian Lock
Electronic programming by Mark Warman

Additional Music by Gerard Schurmann

Souvenir De Florence Op. 70
Adagio Cantabile E Con Moto
Composed by Peter Ilich Tchaikovsky
Adapted for screen by Brian Lock

Hungarian Service Company
Transatlantic Media Associates Limited

Commissioning Editor KRO
Frank Jansen

The Producers wish to especially thank
David Aukin, Bela Bunyik, Janine Hage, Gayle Harbor, László
Helle, Allon Reich, Ryclef Rienstra, Harriet Robinson, Robert
Swaab, Suzanna Taverne,
and
The Mayor and People of Sopron, The Director of Kesthely

Castle, Cleem Calis, Raymond Day, Premila Hoon, Zachary Kleiman, Cedomir Kolar, László Melis, Barry Philp, Liora Reich, Mark Westaway, Simon Channing-Williams.

A Gambler Productions (UK) production
in association with Hungry Eye Lowland (The Netherlands)
and Objektiv Filmstudio (Hungary)

Deze film is tot stand gekomen met de steun van het Nederlands Fonds voor de Film & het Coproduktiefonds Binnenlandse Omroep

This film was supported by
EURIMAGES

Developed with the support of the
EUROPEAN SCRIPT FUND
AN INITIATIVE OF THE MEDIA PROGRAMME
OF THE EUROPEAN UNION

CAMERAS AND LENSES BY ARRI MUNICH